Richard Anthony Proctor

**Easy star lessons**

Richard Anthony Proctor

**Easy star lessons**

ISBN/EAN: 9783337041670

Printed in Europe, USA, Canada, Australia, Japan

Cover: Foto ©ninafisch / pixelio.de

More available books at **www.hansebooks.com**

# EASY STAR LESSONS

BY

RICHARD A. PROCTOR

AUTHOR OF
" HALF-HOURS WITH THE STARS," " HALF-HOURS WITH THE TELESCOPE,"
" A LARGER STAR ATLAS," " THE NEW STAR ATLAS," ETC.

———

NEW YORK
G. P. PUTNAM'S SONS
27 AND 29 WEST 23D STREET
1882

# CONTENTS.

|  | PAGE |
|---|---|
| INTRODUCTION . . . . . . . . . . . . . . | 9 |
| THE STARS FOR JANUARY . . . . . . . . . . . | 23 |
| ” FEBRUARY . . . . . . . . . . | 43 |
| ” MARCH . . . . . . . . . . . . | 63 |
| ” APRIL . . . . . . . . . . . . | 85 |
| ” MAY . . . . . . . . . . . . . | 105 |
| ” JUNE . . . . . . . . . . . . | 123 |
| ” JULY . . . . . . . . . . . . | 141 |
| ” AUGUST . . . . . . . . . . . | 155 |
| ” SEPTEMBER . . . . . . . . . | 171 |
| ” OCTOBER . . . . . . . . . . | 189 |
| ” NOVEMBER . . . . . . . . . . | 211 |
| ” DECEMBER . . . . . . . . . . | 227 |

## LIST OF ILLUSTRATIONS.

|  |  |  | PAGE |
|---|---|---|---|
| Fig. | 1 | Horizons | 11 |
| ,, | 2 |  | 12 |
| ,, | 3 | Star Clock | 18 |
| ,, | 4 | Guardians of the Pole | 19 |
| ,, | 5 | Old Figure of Dragon | 24 |
| ,, | 6 and 7 | Modern Figures | 25 |
| ,, | 8 | Andromeda | 30 |
| ,, | 9 | Pegasus | 31 |
| ,, | 10 | Orion | 45 |
| ,, | 11 | Cetus | 51 |
| ,, | 12 | Taurus | 52 |
| ,, | 13 | Ursa Minor | 63 |
| ,, | 14 | Argo, Canis, Columba | 67 |
| ,, | 15 | Cepheus | 72 |
| ,, | 16 | Part of Cygnus | 87 |
| ,, | 17 | Leo | 90 |
| ,, | 18 | Ancient View of Ursa Minor | 105 |
| ,, | 19 | Cassiopeia | 106 |
| ,, | 20 | Her Chair | 107 |
| ,, | 21 | Virgo | 110 |
| ,, | 22 | Perseus | 126 |
| ,, | 23 | Ophiuchus and Scorpio | 142 |
| ,, | 24 | Bootes and Corona | 159 |
| ,, | 25 | Aquarius, Capricornus, Pisces | 171 |
| ,, | 26 | Aquila | 173 |
| ,, | 27 | Dumb-Bell Nebula | 176 |
| ,, | 28 | Stars of Plough | 192 |
| ,, | 29 | Same 36,000 Years Hence | 193 |
| ,, | 30 | Same 100,000 Years Hence | 194 |
| ,, | 31 | Same 100,000 Years Ago | 194 |
| ,, | 32 | Part of Aquarius | 197 |
| ,, | 33 | ,, ,, | 198 |
| ,, | 34 | Cygnus, Lyra, Vulpecula | 214 |
| ,, | 35 | Auriga | 229 |

# LIST OF STAR MAPS.

|  |  | PAGE |  |  | PAGE |
|---|---|---|---|---|---|
| JANUARY | Northern | 36 | JULY | Northern | 148 |
|  | Southern | 37 |  | Southern | 149 |
|  | Eastern | 40 |  | Eastern | 152 |
|  | Western | 41 |  | Western | 153 |
| FEBRUARY | Northern | 56 | AUGUST | Northern | 164 |
|  | Southern | 57 |  | Southern | 165 |
|  | Eastern | 60 |  | Eastern | 168 |
|  | Western | 61 |  | Western | 169 |
| MARCH | Northern | 78 | SEPTEMBER | Northern | 182 |
|  | Southern | 79 |  | Southern | 183 |
|  | Eastern | 82 |  | Eastern | 186 |
|  | Western | 83 |  | Western | 187 |
| APRIL | Northern | 98 | OCTOBER | Northern | 204 |
|  | Southern | 99 |  | Southern | 205 |
|  | Eastern | 102 |  | Eastern | 208 |
|  | Western | 103 |  | Western | 209 |
| MAY | Northern | 116 | NOVEMBER | Northern | 220 |
|  | Southern | 117 |  | Southern | 221 |
|  | Eastern | 120 |  | Eastern | 224 |
|  | Western | 121 |  | Western | 225 |
| JUNE | Northern | 134 | DECEMBER | Northern | 234 |
|  | Southern | 135 |  | Southern | 235 |
|  | Eastern | 138 |  | Eastern | 238 |
|  | Western | 139 |  | Western | 239 |

# EASY STAR LESSONS.

## INTRODUCTION.

IT is very pleasant to know the stars—to be able, like Milton's hermit, to

> "Sit and rightly spell
> Of every star that heaven doth show."

And it is not at all difficult to learn all the chief star-groups,—or constellations, as they are called,—if only the learner goes properly to work. Perhaps I ought rather to say, if the *teacher* goes properly to work. I remember, when I was a boy about twelve years old, being very much perplexed by the books of astronomy, and the star-charts, from which I tried to learn the stars. There was "Bonnycastle's Astronomy," with a very pretty picture of one constellation,—Andromeda, —in which, if one looked very carefully, one could perceive stars, though these were nearly lost in the carefully shaded picture of the Chained Lady herself. Another book which I found in my father's library showed a series of neat pictures of all the chief constellations, but gave no clear information as to their whereabouts. And the charts which I found were not at all easy to understand, being, in fact, the usual star-charts, which give no information whatever about the places of star-groups *on the sky* of any place or at any time. So that it was only by working my way from the Great Bear to constellations close by it, then to others close by these, and so on, that I slowly learned the chief star-groups. The object of the series of maps in this little book is to remove this difficulty for young astronomers.

The maps are arranged in sets of four, shewing what stars can be seen towards the north, towards the south, towards the east, and towards the west, at a certain convenient hour during every night in the year. This hour varies, night by night. On January 1st, the hour at which the stars shown in the first four maps can be seen in the position shown, will be a quarter past nine in the evening; on January 2, about eleven minutes past nine; on January 3, about seven minutes past nine, and so on, earlier and earlier each night; on January 5, at nine; January 8, at a quarter to nine; January 12, half-past eight; January 16, a quarter past eight; January 20, eight o'clock; January 23, a quarter to eight; January 27, half past seven; and January 31, a quarter past seven; and so forth.

The black part of each map shows the sky as it would be seen by observers living in latitude 40° north, Great Britain, North America and all countries between latitudes 25° and 60° north. This is nearly correct (quite sufficiently so for the purpose of these maps). The United States range in latitude from about 52° to 49° north, and the British Isles from 50° to 59°, an entire range of about 34°; but by far the greater portion of the population of the United States and Canada on one side of the Atlantic, and of the British Isles and the chief European States on the other, occupies the region between the latitudes of New Orleans and Glasgow, say 30° and 56° north latitude. The latitude 40° north is a convenient mid-latitude for the entire range. Maps constructed for that latitude—at least maps intended only to teach young astronomers the constellations—serve quite as well for all latitudes within 15° or 20° on either side of 40°. Only it is necessary to indicate where the horizontal line lies for each limiting latitude, and for one or two intermediate latitudes. Not only, too, are such maps serviceable in that way over a wide range of latitude, but they serve also to illustrate how changes in the observer's latitude affect the aspect of the heavens as seen from the place of observation. The effects of such changes are indeed described verbally in our text-books of astronomy,* but such verbal statements are often misunderstood. The maps of my northern and southern series show what the actual changes are, and also how any one who travels from the latitude (say) of London to that of Paris or Rome, or Naples, or farther south to latitudes corresponding to those of Philadelphia, Louisville, New Orleans, and so forth, may observe very readily, namely, the changing aspect of the northern and southern skies.

The lesson taught by these maps, and capable of being thus readily tested in travel, is that, as we travel northwards the horizon line which at any given hour bounds the northern heavens sinks lower and lower; that is, farther and farther from the north pole of the heavens, revealing more and more stars.

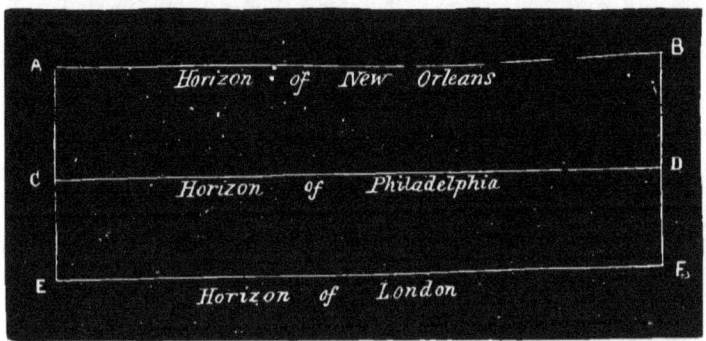

Fig. 1.—Illustrating the position of the northern horizon line among the stars for New Orleans, Philadelphia, and London.

Thus A B. fig. 1, represents the horizon line due north in the latitude of New Orleans (or about 30°); C D, 10° lower

---

* Sometimes not very correctly. For instance, I have seen the remarkable statement made in one Primer of Astronomy that the stars which pass overhead in London "rise and set on a slant,"—the real fact being that they do not rise or set at all, never coming within fully 13° of the horizon.

down among the stars, is the horizon line for Philadelphia and E F, $11\frac{1}{2}°$ lower still, is the horizon for London. In the north then we have in London the advantage of seeing a considerable star region invisible from Philadelphia and other places in the same or nearly the same latitude, and we see a yet larger star region invisible from New Orleans.

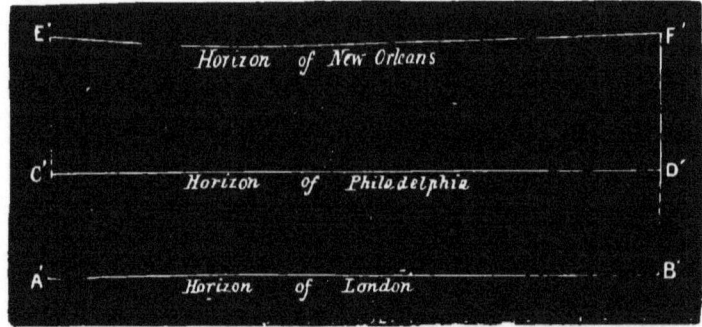

Fig. 2.—Illustrating the position of the southern horizon line among the stars for New Orleans, Philadelphia, and London.

On the other hand, turning towards the south, we find our range of view correspondingly reduced as compared with theirs, the horizon line of Philadelphia lying $11\frac{1}{2}°$ below ours, and that of New Orleans about $21\frac{1}{4}°$ below ours. On the whole, be it noticed, those who reside in lower latitudes have the advantage over us; for the star region we see low down in the north, though invisible to them at the time, yet in due course rises into their view; but the southern star region which they see, and we do not, never rises at all above our horizon.

In the series of northern and southern maps the survey of the heavens is extended from the northern horizon upwards to the point overhead, and thence (in the southern map) downwards to the southern horizon. Since every star seen from any given place on the earth's surface must cross the meridian (or line running from the northern to the southern horizon through the point overhead), these maps show, in fact, every part of the starry heavens visible in the latitudes for which they were made. But although every constellation thus comes under our survey, yet there are some which are not well seen in their full proportions either towards the north or towards the south. Those, for instance, which come exactly overhead when they are crossing the meridian, cannot be drawn in full either in northern or southern maps, because one half of each falls to the north and the other half to the south. They may be seen very well, it is true, when so placed, if the observer lies on his back and looks straight up to the point overhead; but that is not a pleasant way of looking at the sky.

In the eastern and western maps are shown all the constellations which cannot well be shown in northern and southern maps. In this way, we see many star groups which have been learned from northern and southern maps, and moreover every group which is seen in an eastern map will be seen half a year later (or earlier) in a western map. But the position of a constellation is entirely different according as it is seen in an eastern, *southern* or western map, if its course carries it, when at its highest, to the southern skies, or in an eastern, *northern* or western map if its course carries it, when at its highest, to the northern skies. No one can be said thoroughly to know the constellations until he knows them in all the varied aspects which they thus present. For though some star groups, like the Plough, Orion, the Pleiades, and so on, can be recognized in all positions, yet most of them are not so well marked, and when seen in one position might easily be mistaken for new constellations by those who only knew them as seen in another position.

The study of the eastern and western maps forming the present series can either be combined with the study of northern and southern maps, or pursued separately.

All the maps are as true for one year as for another. They will remain true for hundreds of years.

Let it be noticed that the plan on which these eastern and

western maps are drawn is such that every star is shown at its true height above the proper horizon line, and at its true proportionate distance to the right or left of the line from the middle point marked 0° to the proper point overhead for the latitude where the observations are made.

The Eastern and western maps, however, present a different appearance from northern and southern maps. There is a great space under the various horizon lines in these maps, where the stars are shown black on a white ground, to indicate that they are not visible from any of the places for which the series of maps are drawn. They occupy the position shown below the various horizon lines. The horizon lines for other places, instead of lying above or below the horizon of Philadelphia, all pass through the east or west point of this horizon line, but are more or less inclined to it. Then again the point overhead for other places than Philadelphia, instead of lying in the maps above or below the point overhead for Philadelphia, lie to the right or to the left of it in the eastern and western maps. All this corresponds with the reality. If at any given hour on any night you could travel very rapidly many degrees northwards, you would see the northern stars rising, the southern stars sinking, while the eastern and western horizons would seem to move see-saw fashion,—their northern parts dipping so as to show more stars, and their southern parts rising so as to hide stars. On the other hand, if you travelled very rapidly many degrees south, you would see the southern stars rising, the northern sinking: the eastern and western *horizon points* would remain unchanged, and the eastern and western *horizons* would obviously seem to oscillate about the points due east and west, their northern parts rising so as to hide stars, and their southern parts sinking so as to show more stars.

I may add that if you went as far south as the equator, the line marked "equator" in the illustrative maps would come upright in the east and west, so as to form what astronomers call the "prime vertical." On the other hand, if you could go to the north pole, the line marked "equator" would be your horizon line.  You will see, as month after month passes, that the line marked "equator" has an unchanging position in all eastern and in all western maps ; while the line marked "solstitial colure" travels round with the stars, as does also another line marked "equinoctial colure," which, in the maps for May and November, is seen overhead.  These two lines, the equinoctial colure and the solstitial colure, are parts of great circles which pass through the poles of the heavens.

In each map the Latin names of the constellations are given ; but in the description of each map the English names will be given, and a few remarks on each constellation.  The Greek letters used by astronomers are also given ; and the young learner who may not happen to know the Greek alphabet, will do well to learn the names of the Greek letters, as follows :

| | | | |
|---|---|---|---|
| α | Alpha | ν | Nu |
| β | Beta | ξ | Xi |
| γ | Gamma | ο | Omicron |
| δ | Delta | π | Pi |
| ε | Epsilon | ρ | Rho |
| ζ | Zeta | σ | Sigma |
| η | Eta | τ | Tau |
| θ | Theta | υ | Upsilon |
| ι | Iōta | φ | Phi |
| κ | Kappa | χ | Chi (Ki) |
| λ | Lambda | ψ | Psi |
| μ | Mu | ω | Omĕga |

Most of the bright stars have proper names, chiefly derived from the Arabic.  Many of these will be mentioned as our survey proceeds.

The first step toward a knowledge of the stars should be the recognition of the Pole-star ; because the pole of the heavens being the point round which all the stars are seemingly carried, so soon as we know the stars around the pole, we have a centre, so to speak, from which we can pass to other groups until we know them all. Once known, the Pole-star can always be found by the learner, supposing he observes the heavens always from the same station; for it lies always in the same position (or so nearly so that the change can scarcely be noticed). If, for example, you have found that from a certain spot in your garden, or from a certain window in your house, the Pole-star can be seen just above a certain chimney or tree, then at any time, on any night when the sky is clear, if you betake yourself to that spot, or look through that window, you will see the Pole-star over its accustomed chimney or tree. It is there, indeed, all the time, whether the sky be clear or cloudy, whether it be day or night. Not only does a knowledge of the Pole-star give you a known central-point whence to proceed to other stars, but it gives you the means of knowing where lie the cardinal points round the horizon; for, of course, when you face the Pole-star, the north lies before you, the south behind you, the east on your right, the west on your left.

But to find the Pole-star, it is well to begin with the set of stars called in England the Plough, and in America the Dipper. This well-marked group includes two stars which are called the "Pointers," because they point to the pole-star. The Plough or Dipper is so conspicuous and well-marked a group that it is easily learned and cannot easily be forgotten. Although not very near the pole, it is yet not so far from it as to range very widely over the heavens; but if you look toward the north at any hour of any clear night, you will seldom require many seconds to find the familiar set of seven bright stars, though at one time it is high above the pole, at another close to the horizon, now to the right of the pole, and anon to the left. In England the seven stars never set; in America some of them set, but still the group can be recognized (except at stations in the most southern States) even when partly below the horizon.

Let us inquire, first, where the Plough or Dipper is to be looked for, and in what position its stars are placed, at various hours all the year round. Of course, in a general sense, the group lies always *towards* the north. The student, therefore, will not, like " Bird o' Fredum Sawin'," "w'eel roun' about sou'-west" to find it. Still, it saves trouble to have some idea where and how the group will be placed, especially if the night of observation is half clouded, so that all the seven stars are perhaps not seen at once.

The seven stars lie low down to the north (as shown at I in Fig. 3) at about six in the evening of December 21st. They are marked, for convenience of reference, with the Greek letters by which astronomers know them, namely: α (Alpha), β (Beta), γ (Gamma), δ (Delta), ε (Epsilon), ζ (Zeta), and η (Eta). The two stars α and β, which form the side of the Plough farthest from the handle, are called the Pointers, because they point (as the arrow shows) toward the Pole-star, marked 1 in the picture. This star is easily distinguished in the heavens, because it is much brighter than any in its immediate neighbourhood. It is not at the true pole of the heavens, which lies where the two cross-lines of the picture intersect. Consequently, the Pole-star goes round the pole, though in a very small circle ;* it is shown in four different positions, numbered 1, 2, 3, and 4, in Fig. 3. The Greek letter α (Alpha) is assigned to it, because it is the alpha star, or leading star, of the group to which it belongs.

---

\* The actual distance of the Pole-star from the pole is about two and a half times the apparent diameter of the moon ; so that the pole-star appears to go round in a circle having a diameter exceeding five times the apparent diameter of the moon. This is a much smaller circle, however, than most persons would suppose from this description: for the mind unconsciously over-estimates the size of the moon. The three stars forming the belt of Orion will afford a very good idea of the range of the Pole-star around the pole ; the stars to the right and left of the middle star of the belt representing almost exactly the relative positions of the Pole-star on the right and on the left of the pole of the heavens. Or the matter may be thus stated : Orion's belt just about measures the distance between 2 and 4, or between 1 and 3, in Fig. 3. A star placed at the true pole would make, with star at 2 and 4 (Fig 3), a set just like the belt of Orion.

B

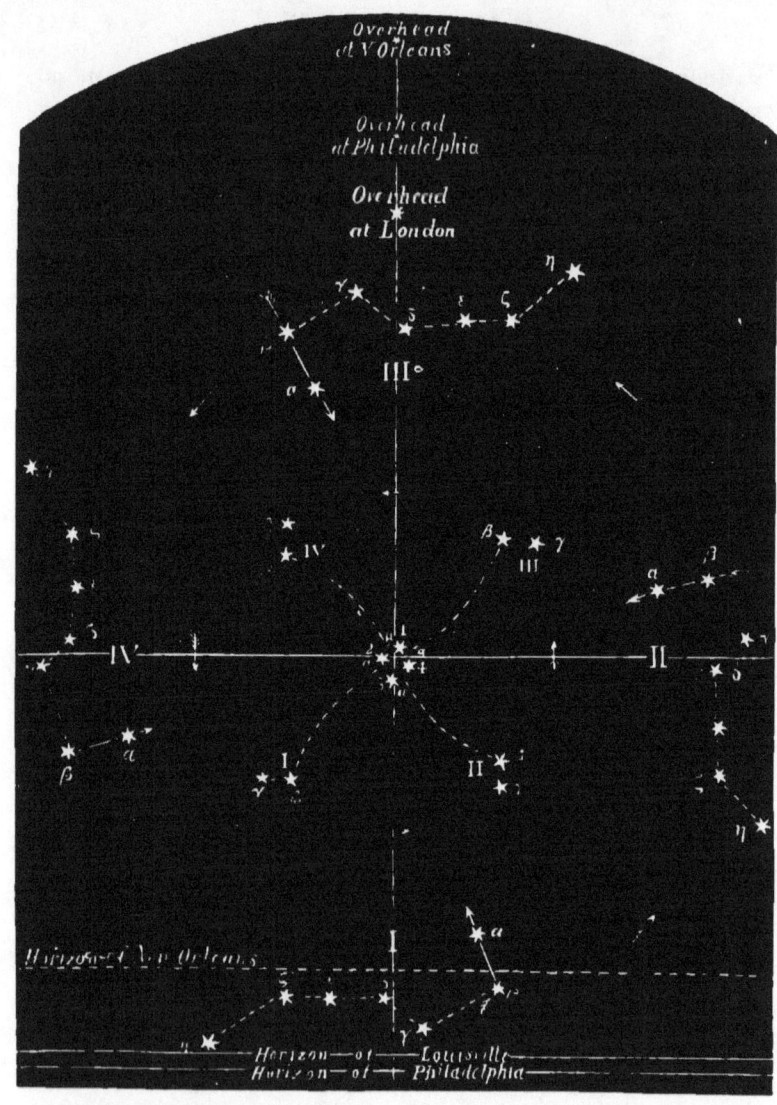

*Horizon of London.*

Fig. 3.—Showing the varying positions of the Plough, the Pole-Star and the Guardians of the Pole, viz. at

I, 1, and I, respectively, at 8 P.M. Nov. 22; at 9 P.M. Nov. 6; at 10 P.M. Oct 22; at 11 P.M. Oct. 6; at midnight Sept. 21.
II, 2, and II, respectively, at 8 P.M. Feb. 19; at 9 P.M. Feb. 5; at 10 P.M. Jan. 21; at 11 P.M. Jan. 5; at midnight Dec. 21.
III, 3, and III, respectively, at 8 P.M. May 21; at 9 P.M. May 8; at 10 P.M April 23; at 11 P.M. April 8; at midnight March 23.
IV, 4, and IV, respectively, at 8 P.M. Aug. 23; at 9 P.M. Aug. 7; at 10 P.M. July 22; at 11 P.M. July 7; at midnight June 22.

The seven stars of the Plough belong to the constellation (or star group) called Ursa Major, or the Greater Bear; while the Pole-star belongs to the constellation called Ursa Minor, or the Lesser Bear. Two other stars, also belonging to Ursa Minor, are shown in the picture, at 1, with their proper Greek letters, β (Beta) and γ (Gamma). They are called the "Guardians of the Pole," because they circle around it as though keeping watch and ward over the axle-end of the great star-dome. The best way, perhaps, to remember where the Guardians are to be looked for, is to notice that the four stars ζ, ε, δ, and β of the Plough are nearly in a straight line, and that if a square be supposed to be set up on this line, as shown in Fig. 4 (on the side toward the pole), the

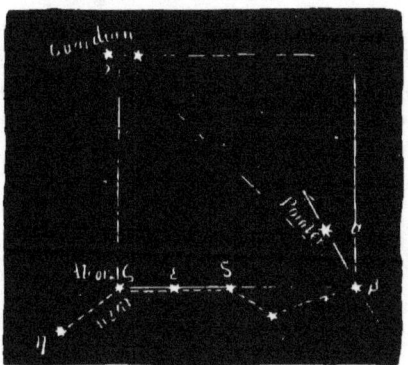

Fig 4.—Showing how the Guardians of the Pole may be found when the Plough is known.

Guardians lie close to that corner of the square which is opposite the pointers. You cannot easily fall into any error as to the four stars of the Plough, or Dipper, to be used in thus finding the Guardians of the Pole, for they are the only four which lie nearly in a straight line. But to make assurance doubly sure, notice that the star ζ, which lies at one end of the line of four stars, has a companion close by (as shown in Fig. 4).* Thus we have at one corner of the square the

* This little star is called by country folks in England "Jack-by-the-Middle-Horse," the stars ε, ζ, and η representing the three horses of

Pointers, at another the double star $\zeta$, and at the next corner the Guardians.

The Plough, as I have said, is in position I at about six o'clock in the evening of December 21st. The Pole-star is at this time placed as at 1, a little above and to the right (or east) of the true pole. The Guardians are at 1. The Plough is now at its lowest; but, as the picture shows, all the seven stars are visible at all places in the latitude of Philadelphia. The dotted line, however, which represents the horizon of New Orleans, shows that in that latitude only one star of the seven can be seen, namely $a$, the pointer nearest to the pole. This star is so bright, that even as far south as New Orleans my description of the position of the Plough will serve as a sufficient guide to find the pole, if only the southerner who uses it notices how Fig. 3 presents the stars of the Plough or Dipper, which for him lie below the horizon. If this method should not suffice, then let him look for the seven stars two hours later, by which time all the other stars except $\zeta$ and $\eta$ will have moved round so far toward position 11 as to be visible at New Orleans,—$\epsilon$ and $\gamma$ lying almost on a horizontal line very near indeed to the horizon.

If on any night toward the end of December, you were to watch the northern heavens from about six o'clock, when the Plough or Dipper is as at I Fig. 3, until about midnight, you would see the group move steadily round till it had reached the position marked II. The Guardians of the Pole would by that time have reached the position II, and the Pole-star, though it would seem to you to be in the same position as at the beginning, would in reality have shifted from 1 to 2.

If you still went on watching, you would find that by about six in the morning the Plough would have gone round in the direction shown by the arrows until it was in the position marked III, high up above the pole and not very far from the point overhead. If your watch had begun earlier in the

the "wain," or wagon. The small star was a test of eyesight among the Arabians. It is, however, very easily seen. The star $\zeta$ is called Mizar, its companion Alcor.

evening, say at about five, when the sky is already quite dark (in December), you would have seen the Plough in a position between I and IV (but nearer to I); and in the course of the entire night,—that is, from evening twilight until daybreak,—the Plough would have gone more than half-way round, from this last-named position to a position somewhat farther round (in the direction shown by the short arrows) than II..

But in order to see the Plough in these different positions, and also in that portion of its course (on either side of IV) which in December it traverses during the daytime, it is not necessary to keep a long watch upon the group, or to study the heavens during those "wee sma' hours ayont the twal" wherein the professional astronomer does the best part of his work. If you come out in the evening (say about eight) once or twice a week on clear nights, all through the winter half of the year, and a little later during the summer months, you will see the Dipper and all the polar groups carried right round the pole. For though, speaking generally, it may be said that they complete a circuit once in every day, yet in reality they gain about four minutes' motion in the twenty-four hours, and thus get further on, little by little, night after night—gaining an hour's motion in about a fortnight, two hours' motion in a month, twelve hours' motion (or half the complete circuit) in half a year, until finally, at the end of the year, they have gained a complete circuit.

Thus at eight o'clock on or about November 22nd, the Plough is at I, the Guardians of the Pole are at I, and the Pole-star is at 1. At eight o'clock on or about February 19th, the Plough is at II, the Guardians are at II, the Pole-star is at 2. At the same hour on or about May 21st, the Plough is at III, the Guardians are at III, the Pole-star is at 3. And lastly at the same hour on or about August 23rd, the Plough is at IV, the Guardians are at IV, the Pole-star is at 4.

It is because of this steady turning motion or rotation around the poles of the heavens, that the stars of the Plough

(say, for instance, the pointers) form as it were a clock\*
in the sky by which an astronomer at any rate, though
also any one who is willing to give a little attention to the
matter, can tell the hour within a few minutes on any night
in the year.

A few observations made in this way on a few nights
during the course of the year, will give a clearer idea of the
steady motion of the star-dome (resulting in reality from the
earth's steady rotation on her axis) than any amount of
description either in books or by word of mouth.

---

\* We find traces in the writings of old times that the stars were used to show the time. For instance, the "first carrier" in Shakspeare's "First Part of King Henry IV." (act ii scene 1) says, "An't be not four by the day, I'll be hanged; Charles' Wain is over the new chimney."—Charles' Wain being the group of seven bright stars which is commonly called in England "the Plough" and in America "the Dipper."

# THE STARS FOR JANUARY.

LOOKING northward (see map, p. 36) we see that Draco (the Dragon) occupies the region due north immediately under Ursa Minor," the Little Bear." The full proportions of the Dragon are clearly and conveniently shewn (except in the southern parts of the United States,—for the horizon of New Orleans conceals from view the two bright stars $\gamma$ and $\beta$, which anciently formed the head of the great monster). In those modern maps which show the constellation figures, the Dragon is represented differently, and generally somewhat as in Fig. 5 (knots and all). But you cannot *imagine* the stars to form a dragon or a snake, in that way. Now we may be sure that the ancients, when they called a group of stars by any name, really imagined some resemblance between the star-group and the figure after which they named it. I have heard it said that the liveliest imagination cannot form figures of familiar objects out of the stars; but this is certainly a mistake, for I know that when I was a lad, and before I had learned to associate the stars with the constellations at present in use, I used to imagine among the stars the figures of such objects as I was most familiar with. In the constellation of the Swan, I saw a capital kite. In the Great Bear I saw the figure of a toy very common at that time in England, representing a monkey that passed over the top of a pole. The three stars forming the handle of the Plough ($\eta$, $\zeta$, and $\epsilon$) made the tail of the monkey; and if you look at the Great Bear in the position it now occupies in the early evening, you will readily see the figure of a climbing monkey, In Perseus I could see a garland of flowers such as my sisters used to make. Orion was a climbing giant in the east,— a giant going down hill as he passed over to the west. In the Serpent-bearer and the Serpent I saw a monstrous sword, shaped like the curved sabre which Saladin wielded and so forth. No doubt, in the infancy of astronomy, or the world itself, men were fanciful in the same way, and the figures

Fig. 5.

they assigned to the star groups really seemed pictured in the heavens. Add to this the consideration that it would not be among the stars overhead, but among those towards the horizon, that they would imagine such shapes, and I think we can understand where and how they saw a dragon in the stars shown in the lower part of our northern map. It was not such a nondescript as Fig. 5 which they saw, but really a snake-like figure; and for my own part I have no doubt whatever that the stars $\beta$ and $\gamma$ were the eyes of the dragon they imagined, and that its head was pictured in their imagination somewhat as shown in Fig. 6.* On referring to the northern map, you will see that I have borrowed a star from Hercules to make the snake's head complete. But that does not trouble my mind in the least. The idea of separating the constellations one from another was a much later one than that of merely naming the more remarkable star-groups. If one set of stars seemed to resemble any object, and another set to resemble another object, I think the corresponding names would have been given even though some stars of one set were included within the other set. In fact this very constellation of the Dragon seems to me to show that our modern constellation figures have been largely reduced in extent. When I look northward at the Dragon placed as in the northern map, I see not a mere snake with his

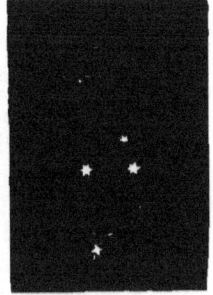

Fig. 6

Fig. 7.

* Aratus, in describing the constellations, speaks of the Dragon as 'with eyes oblique retorted, that askant cast gleaming fire.''

head as in Fig. 5, but a monstrous winged serpent, as in Fig. 7; only, to make the figure complete, I have to take in a large piece from the Little Bear. The stars thus borrowed make a great wing for the Dragon; the stars $\omega$, $\psi$, 15, etc., of the Dragon make another wing; and the neck, body, and tail run from $\zeta$ through $\eta$, $\theta$, $\iota$ and $a$ to $\lambda$.

You may, perhaps, think that it matters very little what figures the ancients really imagined among the stars. But you will be disposed to think differently when I mention that the supposed want of resemblance *now* between the star-groups and the figures assigned to them, has led some to form the bold idea that there was *once* a strong resemblance, but that some stars have gone out, others have shone forth more strongly or are altogether new, and that thus the resemblance has been destroyed. When we remember that our sun is only one among the vast number of suns, it becomes rather a serious matter for the inhabitants of the earth if so many suns have really changed. For, in that case, our sun may soon change in his turn, and either broil us up with excess of heat or leave us to perish miserably from extremity of cold. However, I think the explanation which I have given shows that the resemblance formerly imagined still remains, and that it is only because modern astronomy has docked the dimensions of the old figures that they no longer correspond with their names.

Above the Dragon we see the Lesser Bear, the two Guardians of the Pole, $\beta$ and $\gamma$, having swung round a little past the lowest part of their circuit. Approaching the north from the left are the stars of Cepheus, which will in a month or two be more favourably placed for study. Notice the glory of the "milky way" overhead. Looking that way, also, the very bright star Capella will attract your notice. It belongs to the constellation Auriga, or "the Charioteer." There is a nearly vacant space between Auriga and Ursa Minor, which seems to show that in that direction the system of stars to which our sun belongs is not so richly strewn with suns as elsewhere. And although, when a telescope is turned toward this region, hundreds and thousands of stars are brought into view, yet not nearly so many are seen as when the same telescope is directed toward Perseus or Cassiopeia.

And now turning our back upon the Pole-star, let us look toward the south (see the southern map, p. 37). The mighty river Eridanus occupies nearly the whole space between the equator and the southern horizon. This constellation, which is one of the most ancient star-groups, is a great deal too large; it has not room to turn itself. Observe how poor Bayer (the astronomer who first gave to the stars of each constellation the letters of the Greek alphabet) was perplexed by the large number of stars he had to deal with. There are seven Taus (in reality there are nine but the other two are small), and five Upsilons are shown (out of seven), while several stars which ought to have received their proper Greek letters, have been only numbered.

Above Eridanus is the fine constellation Taurus, or "the Bull," belonging to the zodiacal twelve which mark the road-way of the sun and planets. The sun's path, or ecliptic, is marked on the map, the portion shown being that which he traverses in May and June. The symbol ♊ represents the signs of "the Twins," the sun entering that sign, on his course toward the left shown by the arrow, about the 21st of May—which is, therefore, *not* the time to look for Taurus or the Pleiades, seeing that the sun is shining in the midst of their region of the heavens. The sign of Gemini, used formerly to agree with the constellation of "the Twins," but now, as the map shows, falls upon Taurus.

The group of stars called the Pleiades is one of the most interesting objects in the heavens. In former times they were thought to exert very important influences on the weather, probably because when the sun was in Taurus, which then corresponded with the end of April, it was a time when all Nature seemed to spring into activity.

Admiral Smyth says that the passage in Job, translated, "Canst thou bind the sweet influences of the Pleiades, or loose the bands of Orion?" etc., should be rendered thus :

> "Canst thou shut up the delightful teemings of Chimah?
> Or the contractions of Chesil canst thou open?"

Chimah representing Taurus, or the constellation occupied by the sun (in Job's time) in spring (April and May); while Chesil is not Orion, but Scorpio, the constellation which in Job's time was occupied by the sun in autumn (October and November). It is interesting to notice the ancients thus regarding the stellar influences, as exerted, not when the stars in question are visible in the night-time, but when their rays are combined with those of the sun, which also was the way in which astrologers regarded the stars. Taurus now shines highest in the skies at midnight towards the end of November, but in Job's time six or seven weeks earlier. Hesiod, speaking of their return to the night skies after being lost in the sun's rays, which in his day would be in early autumn, says :

> "There is a time when forty days they lie,
> And forty nights, conceal'd from human eye:
> But in the course of the revolving year,
> When the swain sharps the scythe, again appear."

With the telescope, more than two hundred stars can be seen in this group. To ordinary vision, six only are visible. Yet many persons see seven, not a few can see nine or ten, and Kepler tells us that Moestlin could count no less than fourteen stars, without telescopic aid.

The bright and somewhat ruddy star Aldebaran is in the head of the Bull, formed by the closely clustering group between Aldebaran, $\epsilon$ and $\gamma$. This group is called the Hyades, from a Greek word signifying rain, the influence of these stars being considered showery. The two stars $\beta$ and $\zeta$ form the tips of the bull's horns.

Facing the Bull, we see on the left the glorious constellation Orion. But this constellation is so important that I will defer my account of this splendid group to next month, when, at the hours selected for our evening observations, he shines in full glory upon the meridian.

Let us turn now to the eastern, then to the western skies, to see what star groups are in view there (see maps, pp. 40 and 41).

In the east, we see the three zodiacal constellations—Gemini (the Twins), Cancer (the Crab), and Leo (the Lion); the horns of Taurus (the Bull) can also be seen above Gemini.

Gemini derives its name from the two bright stars—still twin stars in lustre—Castor and Pollux. It is said that Castor was formerly the brighter; but at present Pollux is the brighter, according to Sir J. Herschel's estimate, nearly in the proportion of four to three. Formerly this group was represented by a pair of kids; but the Greeks substituted twin-children with their feet resting on the Milky Way. The Arabian astronomers changed the twins to peacocks; while the astronomers of the Middle Ages substituted two winged angels for the pair. The constellation would perhaps remind one very much of two kids, if it were not so like two angels, or two peacocks, or twin brothers. Gemini is supposed by astrologers to be a sign which rules specially over London. It is also regarded as specially favourable to sailors.

Cancer was called "the dark sign" in old times, because it shows so few stars. But it is full of interest to the telescopist. The fine cluster called Præsepe, or the Beehive, visible to the naked eye only as a faint fleck of luminous cloud, is found, when examined with the telescope, to contain multitudes of stars.

The fine constellation Leo, of which half is visible in the east, at the times named, presents a striking contrast to Cancer, containing many bright stars. The portion shown is commonly called the Sickle in Leo, and is interesting as including the point in the heavens whence the famous November shooting stars, seen in showers on the morning of November 14th, 1833, 1866, &c., seem to radiate. High up in the east is Auriga (the Charioteer), with the bright star Capella, one of the three chief brilliants of the northern heavens, the other two being Arcturus and Vega. The Lesser Dog is seen below, and rather to the left of Gemini. Almost on the horizon of London, and very little raised above the horizon of either Philadelphia or New Orleans, is the solitary star Alphard, in the neck of the Sea-serpent (Hydra).

Turning towards the west, we find the inconspicuous zodiacal constellation Pisces (the Fishes), below which can be seen a small part of Aquarius (the Water-bearer). Above Pisces we see Aries (the Ram). The leading constellations in the west are, however, Andromeda (the Chained Lady),

Fig. 8.—Andromeda and Lacerta.

and Pegasus (the Winged Horse). It will be observed that the attitude of Pegasus, as he is at present seen in the west, is not precisely that which we expect a horse to occupy, even if he has wings permitting of his assuming other varieties of position than are usual among ordinary horses.

Neither is Andromeda in the attitude customarily adopted by ladies. We thus see illustrated the necessity of studying the constellations in all the positions they can assume. Owing to the precession of the equinoxes, the constellations Andromeda and Pegasus, like most others, are so situated that they no longer assume, in any part of our heavens, the natural positions which, when they were first invented, they occupied in one part at least of their revolution. But they still assume positions much more nearly corresponding with the proper attitude of the figures they are supposed to represent. If these constellations were only learned as so figured, the student would not recognise them at all in such attitudes as they have at present. Their supposed figures are somewhat as represented in Figs. 8 and 9.

# STAR MAPS FOR JANUARY.

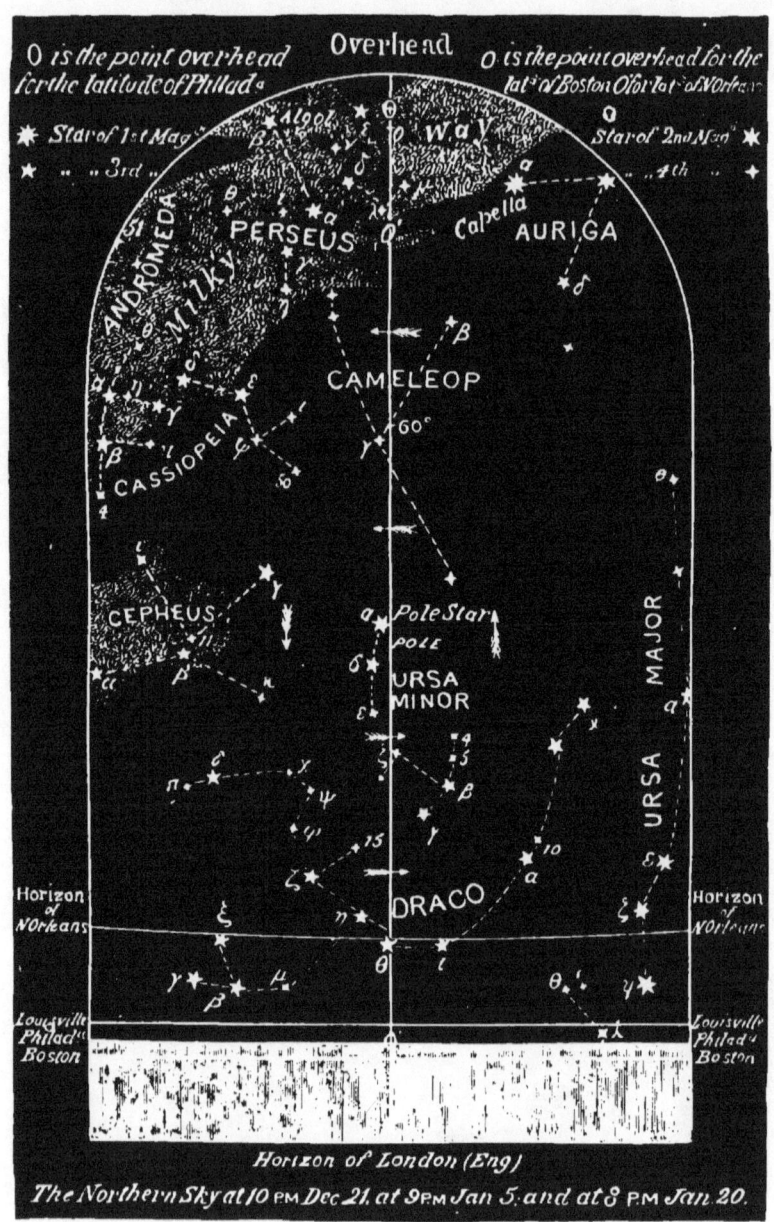

THE NORTHERN MAP FOR JANUARY.

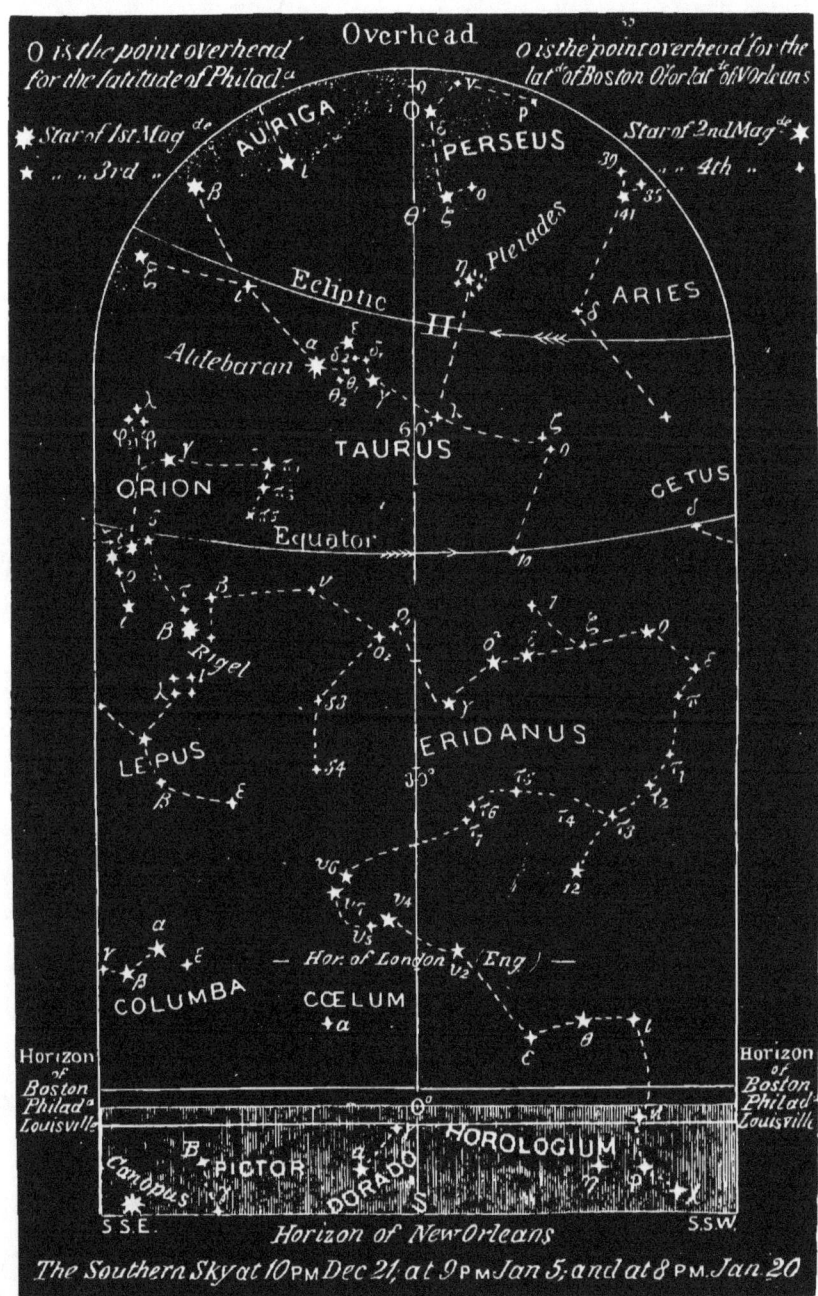

THE SOUTHERN MAP FOR JANUARY.

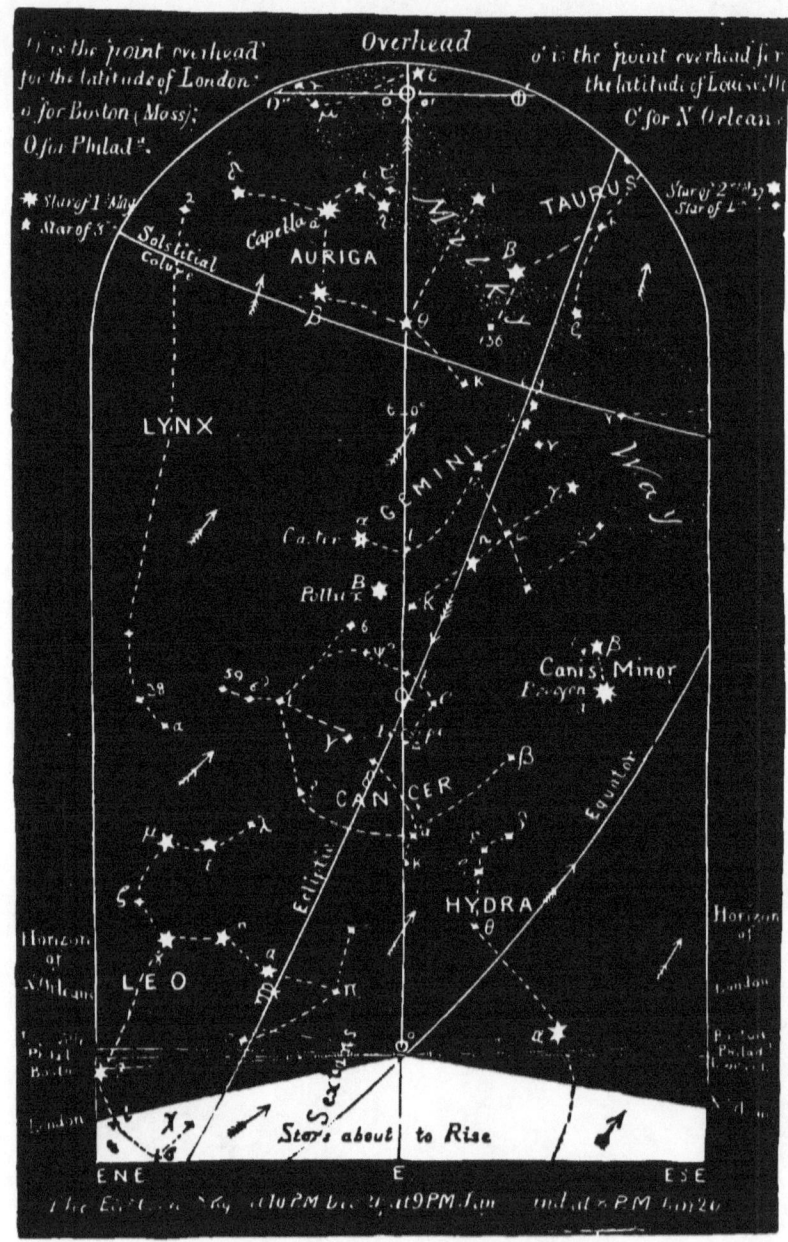

THE EASTERN MAP FOR JANUARY.

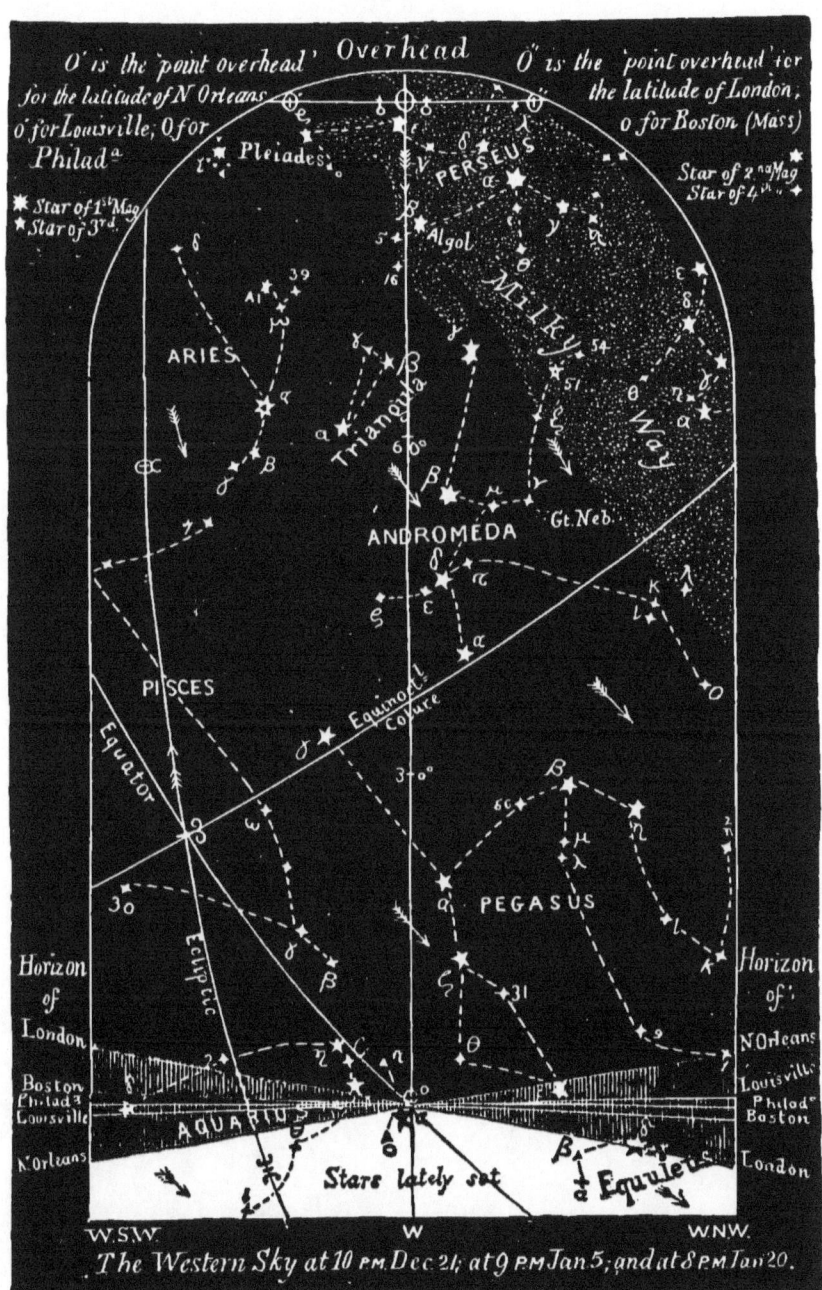

THE WESTERN MAP FOR JANUARY.

# THE STARS FOR FEBRUARY.

THE northern heavens (map, p. 56) present no change of special importance since last month. The Dragon has been carried away from his former *hovering* position, and now appears as if swooping downward, though in a direction contrary to that of his real motion around the pole. The ancient observers do not seem to have attached any importance, by the way, to the direction in which the star-sphere turns; and, indeed, a motion so slow as not to be perceptible by ordinary vision might well be left out of account in forming imaginary star-groups. Some of the figures go forward, as Orion, the Great Bear, Boötes (the Herdsman), the Lion, and so forth; others go backward, as the Dragon, the Ram, the Bull, Pegasus (the Winged Horse), and so on; while others, like Ophiuchus (the Serpent-bearer), are supposed to face the observer and so travel sideways; and others again, travel on their head, as Hercules, Cepheus, and Andromeda. It is quite clear that those who invented the constellation figures did not trouble themselves much about the rotation of the star-vault.

There may be noticed in the northern heavens, as seen in February, a vacant space above the pole, girt round by the constellations Auriga (the Charioteer) overhead, Perseus (the Rescuer), Cassiopeia (the Seated Lady), Cepheus (her royal husband), and the two Bears. In this poverty-stricken region there are no stars of the first three magnitudes, and only four or five of the fourth magnitude. The ancient astronomers could imagine no constellations in these spaces. It is to the moderns, and especially to Hevelius, that we owe the constellations which have been figured in these barren districts. The Camelopard, or Giraffe, is one; the Lynx another. I cannot say, for own my part, that I see either a giraffe or a lynx there. Certainly, if you draw the connecting lines shown in the map, you get as fair a picture of a giraffe (inverted at present) as can possibly be made with a couple of lines; but it seems to me—though I do not claim to be an artist—that rather more than two lines are needed to picture a respectable giraffe. Besides, the lines are not on the sky, and the liveliest fancy would not think of connecting these stars by imaginary lines, so widely remote are the stars, and so insignificant.

The Little Bear is now gradually getting round (at the selected hour of evening observation) to a position such as a bear might reasonably assume. Last month, this small bear was hanging head downward by the end of his absurdly long tail. He is now slowly rising from that undignified position, and by next month he will have fairly placed himself on his feet. For the present we can leave him to his struggles; but next month we shall consider his history and the duties which he has discharged for many hundreds of years.

Turning to the southern skies (p. 57), we find full compensation for the relatively uninteresting aspect of the northern heavens. The most resplendent constellation in the heavens is now in full glory in the south. There, close to the meridian, or mid-south,

> " Begirt with many a blazing star,
> Stands the great giant Algebar,
> Orion, hunter of the beast:
> His sword hangs gleaming by his side,
> And on his arm the lion's hide
> Scatters across the midnight air
> The golden radiance of its hair."

No one can mistake this most beautiful **constellation**

The two bright shoulder stars, Betelgeux (α) and Bellatrix (γ), the brilliant star Rigel on the giant's advanced foot, the triply gemmed belt (ζ, ε, and δ), and the pendent sword tipped with the bright star ι, distinguish Orion unmistakably. But, besides these glories, there are others; the

Fig. 10.—Orion.

curve of small stars forming the giant's shield (a lion's hide), the misty light of the great nebula which lies on the sword (where shown), and on clear nights the dappled light of the Milky Way, which really extends over a part of this constellation, to say nothing of numbers of faint stars scattered all over it, justify the words of the poet, who sang:

> "Orion's beams! Orion's beams!
>   His star-gemmed belt, and shining blade;
> His isles of light, his silvery streams,
>   And gloomy gulf of mystic shade."

From the beginning of astronomy, and probably long before astronomy was thought of, this constellation was figured as a giant: sometimes a giant hunter, a sort of celestial Nimrod; sometimes as a warrior. He commonly wields an immense club in his right hand (the star $\nu$ marks the handle of the club), and a shield (formed by the stars $\pi_1$, $\pi_2$, etc.) in his left. The star $\beta$ of the constellation Eridanus really marks the giant's bent knee; and originally the constellation Lepus, or "the Hare," formed a chariot in which the hunter or warrior stood. In some old manuscripts of the Middle Ages, the stars of Lepus formed a throne for Orion. In fact, this little constellation, although named the Hare from time immemorial, has been called by other names, insomuch that Ideler, after quoting several, wrathfully adds, "And God knows how many more there are."

Fig. 10 shows Orion as he is now generally pictured. He is somewhat out of drawing, because of the necessity of keeping certain stars in particular positions with respect to him. Thus Betelgeux is derived from the Arabic *ibt-al-jauzá*, the giant's shoulder; Bellatrix, or "the Amazon star," belongs of right to the other shoulder, and Rigel to the advanced foot, while the three stars of the belt fix the position of the giant's waist. To tell the truth, he is an ill-shaped giant, any way, and cannot be otherwise depicted.

Below Lepus (the Hare) you see the neat little group Columba, or "the Dove." This is one of the younger constellations, and was invented by Hevelius, perhaps to show that the ship Argo, which you see low down on the left, is no other than Noah's Ark. In fact, the name given to the small group originally was Columba Noachi, or "Noah's Dove." Approaching the mid south, you now see the brightest star in the whole heavens—Sirius, the famous Dog-star. The constellation Canis Major (the Greater Dog) which might much better be called simply Canis, was one of Orion's hunting-dogs, Canis Minor being the other ; but we can hardly suppose Lepus was the sole prey pursued by so great a giant and two such fine dogs. The constellation Canis Major is chiefly remarkable for the Dog-star. In old times this star was thought to bring pestilence. Homer speaks of it (not by name, however) as the star

> " Whose burning breath
> Taints the red air with fevers, plagues and death."

Many among the ancients supposed that this star was in reality as large as the sun. Thus Manilius said :

> "'T is strongly credited this owns a light
> And runs a course not than the sun's less bright :
> But that, removed from sight so great a way,
> It seems to cast a dim and weaker ray."

It has been shown in our own time, however, that even this estimate, which was by many thought too daring, falls far short of the truth. It has been calculated that Sirius gives out two hundred times as much light (and doubtless two hundred times as much heat) as our sun. So that it would make us rather uncomfortable if our sun were removed and Sirius set in its place. Sir W. Herschel says that when he turned his large four-feet mirror on this star, the light was like that of the rising sun, and it was impossible to look at the star without pain to the eye. Sirius is in reality in rapid motion, though owing to his enormous distance he seems at rest. He is rushing through space at the rate of about thirty miles in every second of time ! In a year he traverses nearly six times the distance which separates our earth from the sun. But this enormous annual journey is only about $\frac{1}{170000}$th part of the distance which separates him from our earth; and as he is travelling away from us, we need not be greatly troubled on account of him. He is so far from us that his light has been no less than twenty years on its way to us, so that in reality, instead of saying we see Sirius, we ought to say we see where Sirius *was* some twenty years ago. Most of the stars are even farther away, so that if every one of them were in a single instant destroyed, we should still see them—that is, their light—for many years, and probably the greater number of them would still seem to be shining in the heavens long after the youngest of us were dead; perhaps even after our great-grandchildren had passed away.

Canis Minor (the Lesser Dog) is a much less important star-group than Canis Major, but still it is one of the ancient constellations. Its chief star is called Procyon, or "the Fore-dog," because his star is seen as a morning star earlier than Sirius. The Arabian astronomers gave it a name of similar meaning, to wit, *Al-kelb-al-mutekaddem;* but I think Procyon sounds almost as well, and as it is the name by which the star is usually called, it may, perhaps be better to use it instead of the Arabian name, though this is very pretty. Procyon, like Sirius, was supposed to be a star of evil omen, especially as bringing bad weather. "What meteoroscoper," said Leonard Digges, the astrologer, "yea, who that is learned in matters astronomical, noteth not the great effects at the rising of the star called the *Litel Dogge?*"

The constellation Gemini, or the Twins, is now approaching the south, but will be more fully within the range of our next monthly map. The sign marked ♋ is that of Cancer, or the Crab, which the sun enters at midsummer. You will observe that we have now reached the part of the ecliptic highest above the equator, which is, of course, the part reached by the sun at midsummer. The point marked ♋ is at its highest in the south at noon on or about June 21st, and is then occupied by the sun; it is at its highest in the south at midnight on or about December 20, and the sun is then exactly opposite to this point, or at his lowest below the northern horizon.

Those who live as far south as New Orleans, see, well raised above the horizon, the star Canopus, in the stern of the good ship Argo. There is presented to them, at this season, a view of more first magnitude stars than can be seen at any other time in one quarter of the heavens. For besides the splendid equal-sided triangle formed by Procyon, Betelgeux, and Sirius, they see Aldebaran, Rigel, and Canopus, the last-named surpassing every star in the heavens except Sirius alone.

Next month, the great ship Argo will have come better into view; and I defer till then my account of this fine constellation.

The eastern and western maps for this month (pp. 60 and 61), when compared with those for January, show how the stars, observed at any given hour month after month, change in position just as though they were watched hour after hour on the same night. Thus in the January eastern map the Lion is seen low down, and the arrows scattered over the map, which (except the arrow on the ecliptic) point the way the stars are apparently moving, show that the Lion is passing upwards and slightly towards the right, or to just such a position as the constellation has in the eastern map for this month. In fact, if the stars had been observed in January two hours after the time when the Lion was placed as shown in the January map, it would have been found that the Lion had reached the exact position occupied by the constellation in our present map. Two hours' motion on any given night produces the same change of position as one month's motion for stars seen at any given hour. This remark applies to all stars; and the young student will do well to compare together the two eastern maps and the two western maps (for January and February), following up the work by noting month after month how the star groups rise up from out of the eastern horizon, and pass down towards the western. Also he will find it interesting to notice how six months hence the stars which are now rising at any given hour in the east will be found at the same hour setting in the west; while those which at any hour are now setting in the west will be found six months hence rising in the east. What is true of the present time, and six months from the present time, is true of any part of the year, and six months before or after that time.

In the east we see that at the hours named under the map (and of course at intermediate hours on the intermediate dates) the constellation Auriga has passed overhead, leaving only two stars visible in the space covered by the map, and even those two ($\beta$ and $\theta$) have passed over to the western side of the north and south line overhead. The Lion is now the chief constellation of the east; and the student will do well to study it there, for this group is not so well seen at any other part of the year. When in the south, indeed, it is better placed for the astronomer, who cannot have the stars too high above the horizon. But the general student of the skies can note the shape of star groups more conveniently when they are at a moderate elevation.

I think few can recognize in the constellation Leo, as now figured, the shape of a lion. The stars $\mu$, $\epsilon$, and $\lambda$ now mark the place of the lion's head, while his tail ends at the star $\beta$, and his forepaws reach from $\pi$ to $o$. It requires a strong imagination to see a lion among these stars. (See further on, fig. 16.) But I think a much larger lion can be readily seen, the head lying in Cancer, the mane reaching to Leo Minor, the forepaws on the stars $\zeta$, $\epsilon$, and $\delta$, which mark the head of Hydra (the Sea-Serpent), and the hinder paws on the stars $\beta$ and $\zeta$ of Virgo. It seems to me likely that originally the constellations named after men, animals, and other objects, were not, as now, separated from each other; but that if any group, large or small, seemed to resemble any object it was named after that object, whether it formed part or not of another group already named, or whether it included part of such a group or was itself partly included in another constellation.

Of Virgo, which is just beginning to rise above the horizon, I shall have more to say next month.

In the west Pegasus, which was nearly in full view last month, has almost wholly set. Andromeda (still head downwards) is following the Winged Horse, but not towards the same part of the horizon. Perseus, or "the Rescuer," who was overhead last month, now lies between Andromeda and the point overhead, while Auriga (the Charioteer) now occupies the highest region in the heavens.

Two interesting constellations, which last month could not be seen in the western map, have now passed within its precincts, namely, Taurus (the Bull), and Cetus (the Sea Monster or Whale). (Figs. 11 and 12.)

It is very easy to identify the Bull, first by the Pleiads, and, secondly, by the bright and somewhat ruddy Aldebaran. The famous cluster—the so-called *seven* Pleiads—in reality contains an immense number of stars, forming a very beautiful and amazing object when examined even with a small telescope. It is fabled that there were once seven Pleiads visible to the naked eye, but that one, called the lost Pleiad, has faded from view. With good eyesight, however, not only can the original seven Pleiads be distinctly seen, but several others. A few observers have even seen as many as fourteen Pleiads.

The star o (Omicron) Ceti is perhaps the most interesting

star in the heavens. It is shown, in the map, of the second magnitude, but it is in reality variable. At its brightest it shines as a star of the second magnitude; but it only shines thus for about two months out of ten. For about a fortnight it shines as a star of the second magnitude, then by degrees it fades away, until at the end of three months it can hardly be seen. After remaining about five months invisible, it gradually increases in brightness for about three months, when it is again a second magnitude star. It occupies about 331 days 8 hours in going through these changes.

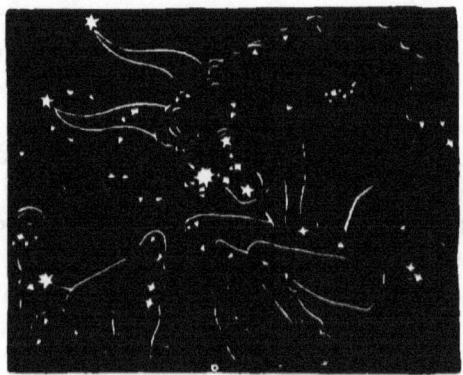

Fig. 12.—Taurus.

# STAR MAPS FOR FEBRUARY.

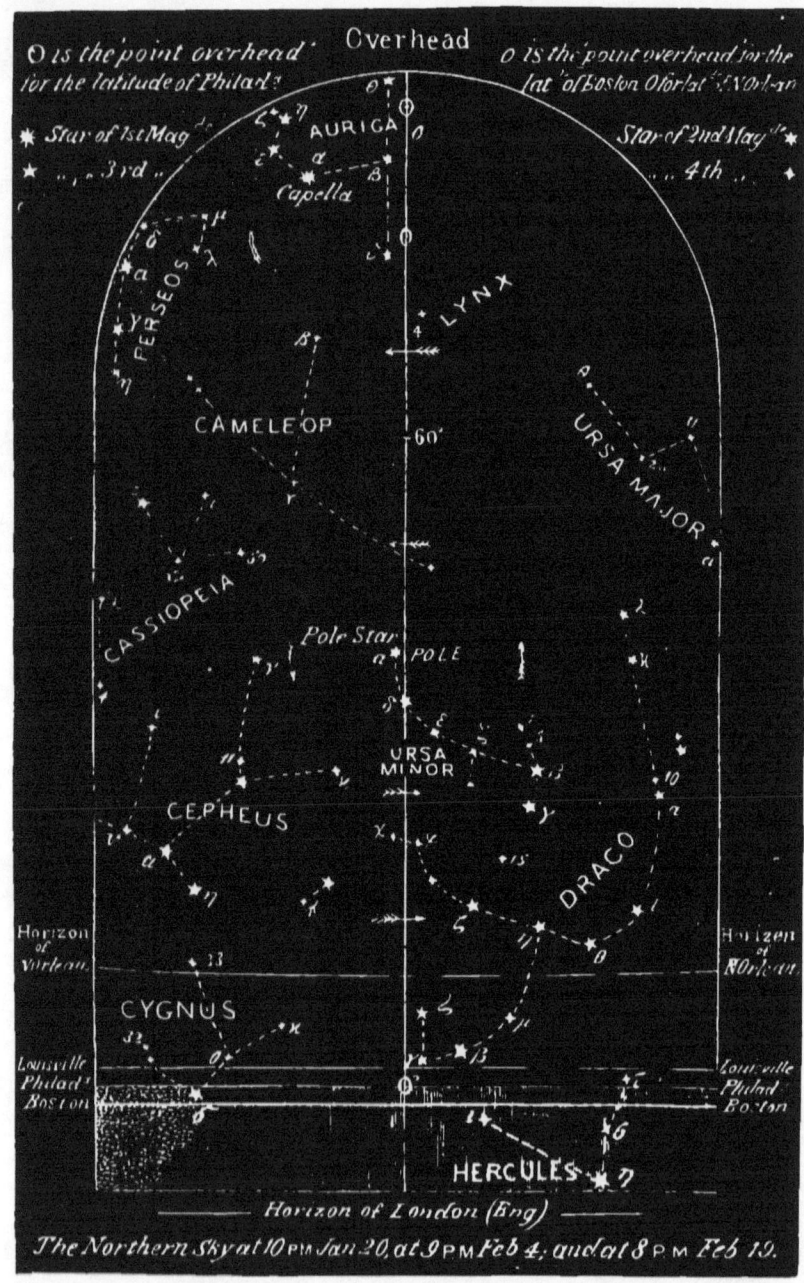

THE NORTHERN MAP FOR FEBRUARY.

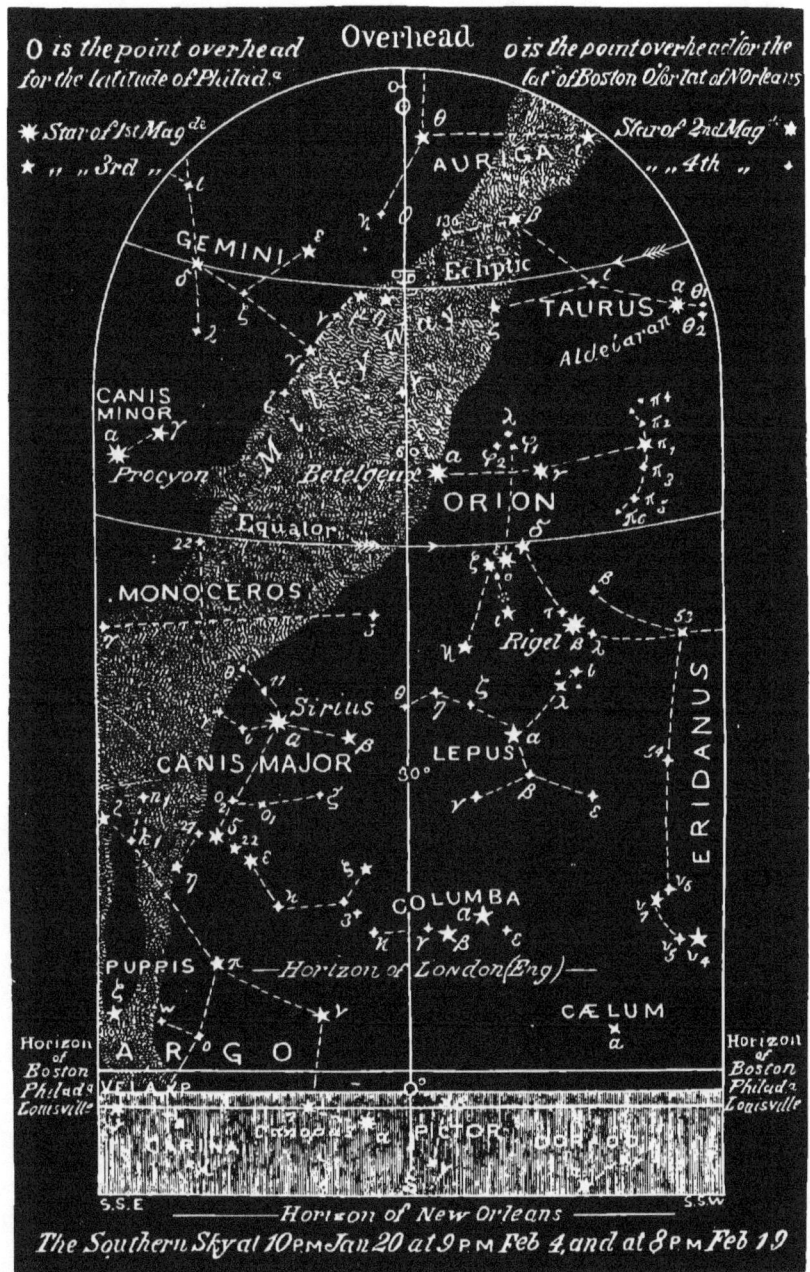

THE SOUTHERN MAP FOR FEBRUARY.

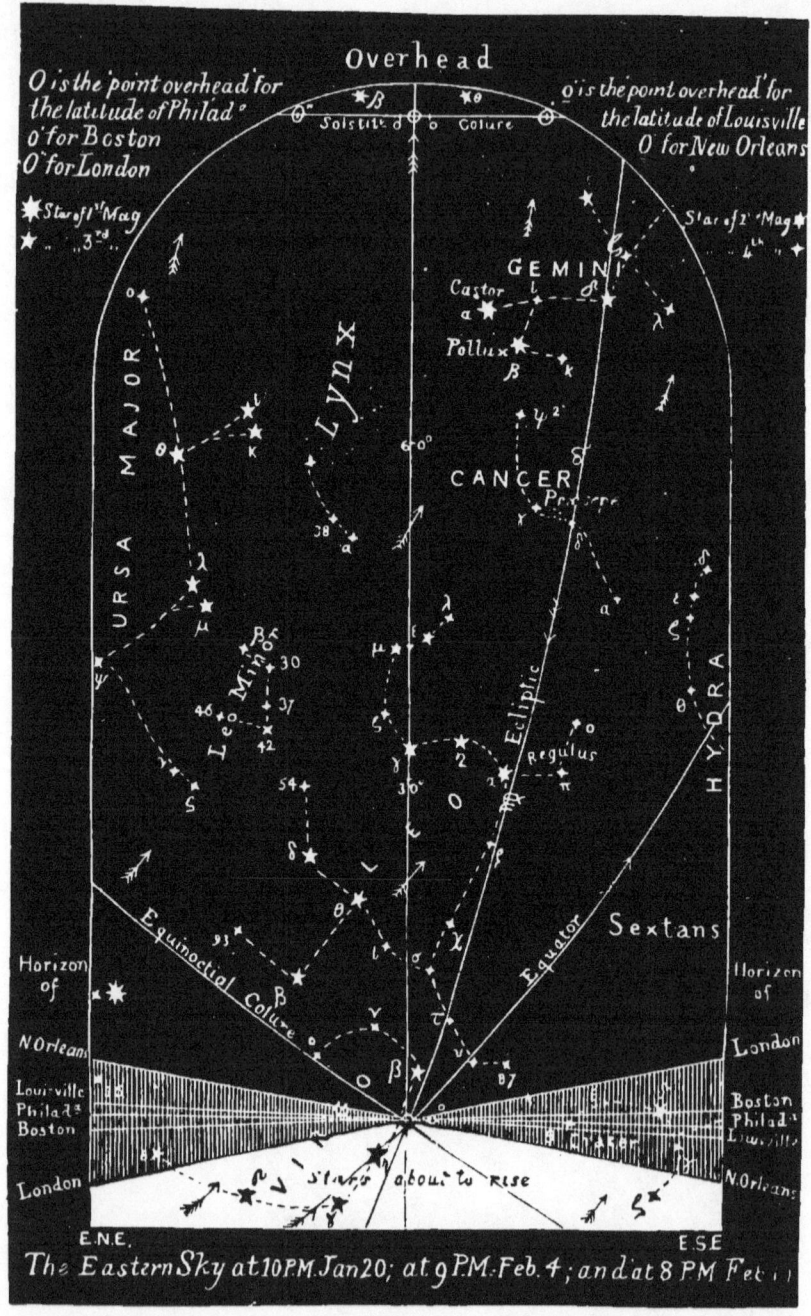

THE EASTERN MAP FOR FEBRUARY.

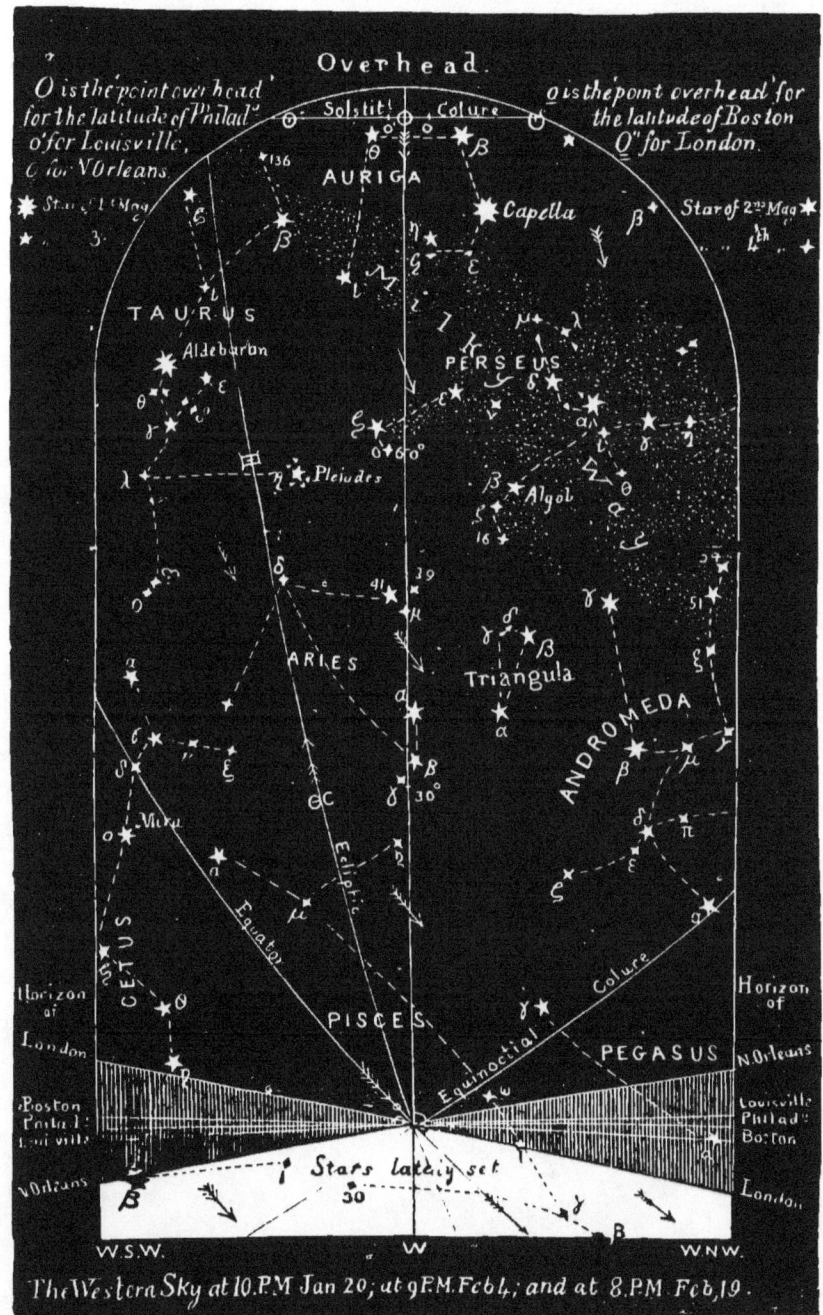

**THE WESTERN MAP FOR FEBRUARY**

# THE STARS FOR MARCH.

URSA MAJOR is now (p. 78) swinging round toward the highest part of his course above the pole. It is his forepaw that you see, marked by the letters θ, κ, and ι, very nearly above the pole; while α and β are the "Pointers" whose motion has been already described.

The Little Bear is nearly in a horizontal position, and I proceed to give a short account of this small but most interesting constellation.

I do not think that the Little Bear, like the larger one, was so named because of any imagined resemblance to a bear. (See Fig. 13.) The original constellation of the

Fig. 13.—Ursa Minor.

Great Bear was much older than the Little Bear, and so many different nations agreed in comparing the group to a bear, that there must have been a real resemblance to that animal in the constellation as first figured. Later, when star-maps came to be arranged by astronomers who had never seen bears, they supposed the three bright stars forming the handle of the plough to represent the tail of the bear, though the bear is not a long-tailed animal. They thus set three stars for the bear's tail, and the quadrangle of stars forming the plough itself for the bear's body. This done, it was natural enough that, seeing in the group of stars now forming the Little Bear the three stars $a$, $\delta$, and $\epsilon$ on one side, and the quadrangle formed by the stars $\zeta$, $\eta$, $\beta$, and $\gamma$ on the other, they should call this group the Little Bear, assigning the three stars to his tail and the quadrangle to his body. Thus did the constellation of the Little Bear probably take its rise. It was not formed by fanciful folks in the childhood of the world, but by astronomers. Yet it must not be imagined that the constellation is a modern one. It not only belongs to old Ptolemy's list, but is mentioned by Aratus, who borrowed his astronomy from Eudoxus, who "flourished" (as the school-books call it) about 360 years before the Christian era. It is said that Thales formed the constellation, in which case it must have reached the respectable age of about 2,500 years. It is usually pictured as shown in Fig. 1, and a very remarkable animal it is.

But if the Little Bear is not a very fine animal, it is a most useful constellation. From the time when the Phœnicians were as celebrated merchant-seamen as the Venetians afterward became, and as the English-speaking nations now are, this star-group has been the cynosure of every sailor's regard. In fact, the word "cynosure" was originally a name given either to the whole of this constellation or to a part of it. Cynosure has become quite a poetical expression in our time, but it means literally "the dog's tail;" and either the curved row of stars $a$, $\delta$, $\epsilon$, $\zeta$, and $\beta$ was compared to a dog's tail, or else the curved row of stars 4, 5, $\beta$, and $\gamma$. I incline, for my own part, to think these last formed the true cynosure—for this reason simply, that when the constellation was first formed these stars were nearer the pole than was our present Pole-star. Even in the time of Ptolemy, the star $\beta$ was nearer the pole than $a$, and was called in consequence by the agreeable name Al-Kaukab-al-shemali, which signifies "the northern star." (For the reason why the fixed stars thus changed in position with regard to the pole of the heavens, I must refer you to books on astronomy. I only note here that the star-sphere remains the same all the time; but the earth, which is whirling on its axis like a mighty top, is also *reeling* like a top, and just as the axis of a top is swayed, now east now west, now north now south, so does the axis of the earth vary in position as she reels. I may add that the reeling motion is very much slower than the whirling motion. The earth whirls once on her axis in a day, but she only reels round once in 25,868 years.)

Admiral Smyth gives some interesting particulars about the two stars $\beta$ and $\gamma$, called the Guardians of the Pole. "Recorde tells us," he says, "in the 'Castle of Knowledge,' nearly three hundred years ago, that navigators used two pointers in Ursa—'which many do call the Shafte, and others do name the Guardas, after the Spanish tonge.' Richard Eden, in 1584, published his 'Arte of Navigation,' and therein gave rules for the 'starres,' among which are special directions for the two called the Guards, in the mouth of the 'horne,' as the figure was called." (The Pole-star would mark the small end of the horne.) "In the 'Safeguard of Saylers' (1619) are detailed rules for finding the hour of the night by the 'guardes." 'How often,' says Hervey, in his "Meditations," have these stars beamed bright intelligence on the sailor and conducted the keel to its destined haven!"

The constellation Cepheus is now about to pass below the pole. The royal father of Andromeda is presented in a somewhat unkingly attitude at present—standing, to wit, upon his royal head. In any case, the constellation is not very like a crowned king. The stars $\zeta$, $\epsilon$, and $\delta$ form his head. (A London cockney might find an aid to the memory by noting that these letters $z$, $e$, and $d$ spell, after a sort, " 'iz 'ed ; " but I think young folks in America can hardly imagine the utter demoralization of cockney aspirates.) The constellation Cepheus was probably simply fitted in, that the history of the sacrifice and rescue of Andromeda might be complete; we have Cepheus and Cassiopeia, her father and mother, on one side, and, as will be seen later, Andromeda herself, and her rescuer, Perseus, on the other. But of all the figures, Cassiopeia alone seems suggested by the stars themselves; or rather a chair is suggested, and imagination readily suggested a lady seated therein. Why Cassiopeia, rather than any other lady from Eve downward, is not apparent.

Turning to the southern heavens (p. 79), we find that a remarkable change has taken place since last month. Orion has passed over toward the south-west, whither the Greater Dog is following him; and where Orion stood in full glory last month, there is now a singularly barren region. Not only are no stars of the first four magnitudes visible between Hydra and the Milky Way, but over a large portion of this space there is not a single star visible to the naked eye; insomuch that an ingenious Frenchman named M. Rabache was led to suppose that there is here a monstrous dark body millions of times larger than the sun, and hiding from view stars which really lie in this direction. He even went so far as to assert that when the sky was very clear he had discerned the circular outline of this great body,*—the centre, he said, round which all the stars are

---

* I heard of a similar case not a hundred miles from Louisville. A philosopher whose theories required that a planet should travel closer to the sun than Mercury, and who had somehow calculated that such a planet supposed to have been seen by a Frenchman named Lescarbault in March, 1859, would pass across the sun's face in a certain September, succeeded in seeing it there. Subsequent calculation showed, unfortunately, that the planet, if it exists at all, would indeed have then

travelling. But unfortunately for our faith in this little story, the telescope shows multitudes of small stars scattered over the whole of this region.

Fig. 14.—The constellations, the Great Ship Argo, Canis Major, and Columba.

The constellation Argo, or the Great Ship (Fig. 14), now occupies the region immediately above the southern horizon. This constellation is not at all well seen in England, or even (as you can see from the way in which the horizon line of the latitude of Philadelphia divides it) in the greater part of the United States. Only when the latitude of New Orleans is approached does the keel of the ship, and the bright star Canopus in the rudder (or guiding oar), show out well

lain in the same direction as the sun, but beyond him, not on this side of him! An old proverb says that certain persons should have good memories; it is at least equally true that one who proposes to invent an observation should be a correct computer.

above the horizon. But, to say the truth, this fine celestial ship nowhere represents in these days the ship-shape appearance which it had some three thousand years ago. The same cause which has shifted the position of the poles of the heavens, has tilted Argo up by the stern, until she resembles rather one half of a vessel which has been broken on a ridge of rocks, than as she was formerly described, "the stern half of a vessel drawn poop foremost into harbour." I have drawn her in Fig. 14 as she was placed three thousand years ago. You have only to tilt the picture sideways a little, until Sirius on the Dog's nose is above Canopus, to place the constellation as it now appears above the southern horizon. I believe that in reality the old constellation, besides being better placed, was much larger than the present. The fine group of clustering stars now covering the Dove and the hind-quarters of the Dog, belonged, I think, to the stern of Argo. In fact, these stars form the well-marked outline of one of the old-fashioned lofty poops. The Dove, by the way, is a well-placed little constellation; but the Dog, prancing just behind the stern of Argo, forms an altogether incongruous element in the picture. On account of its great size the constellation Argo is divided. We have Puppis, the poop or stern; Malus, the mast; Vela, the sails; Carina, the keel. Not to confuse the picture by many lines I have not shown the outlines of these parts. In fact it can only be properly shown in a regular star-atlas. (In Map V. of my school star-atlas for schools these sub-divisions are shown.) Only it is to be noticed that while the Greek letters refer to the whole ship, the italic and Roman letters refer to the various parts. Thus the stars marked $\rho$ and $\zeta$ (on the summit of the stern) would be called respectively $\rho$ Argûs and $\zeta$ Argûs, but the stars close by marked $k_1$ and $n_1$ would be called $k$ Puppis and $n$ Puppis, and so on.

The part of the Milky Way occupied by Argo is remarkable for its singularly complex shape. It is well to notice how incorrect is the ordinary description of the Milky Way as a zone of cloudy starlight circling the entire heavens. Here you see it spreading out into a great fan-shaped expansion, separated from a somewhat similar one by a wide dark space.

Above the equator, two zodiacal constellations are seen,—the fine constellation Gemini, or "the Twins," the poor one Cancer, or "the Crab." Cancer used to be the sign in which the sun attained his greatest elevation in summer, or rather it was as he entered this sign that he was at his highest. But you see from the map that all the way through the part of Gemini shown, and onward through Cancer, the sun's course is down-hill,—or, in other words, it is after midsummer that he traverses these constellations. The sign ♌ marks the beginning of the zodiacal sign of the Lion.

The constellation Gemini no doubt derived its name from the two stars, nearly equal in lustre, Castor and Pollux. Of these, Castor was formerly the brighter, but now Pollux is brighter, nearly in the proportion of four to three. Formerly, as I have already mentioned, this star-group was represented by a pair of kids; but the Greeks substituted twin-children with their feet resting on the Milky Way; the Arabian astronomers, in their turn, changed the twins to peacocks; and the astronomers of the Middle Ages pictured the twins as two winged angels.

Gemini is said by astrologers to be the sign specially ruling over London, though why this should be so they do not tell us. We can understand why sailors should regard the sign as propitious to them, for when the sun is in Gemini the seas are usually calm,—at least summer is more pleasant for sailors than winter. You will remember that the ship in which Paul sailed from Malta had for its sign the twin brothers Castor and Pollux.

As the Twins pass over towards the west, hour by hour, or night by night at the same hour, they come into the position described by Tennyson, where he sings of

> "a time of year,
> When the face of night is fair* on the dewy downs,
> And the shining daffodil dies, and the Charioteer
> And starry Gemini hang like glorious crowns
> Over Orion's grave low down in the west."

Cancer is a very poor constellation to the eye, but full of interest to the telescopist. Even with a very small telescope, the little cluster called Præsēpe, or "the Beehive," is found to be full of stars. Galileo, whose best telescope was but a poor one, counted thirty-eight stars in this cluster, which to the naked eye looks like a mere fleck of faintly-luminous cloud.

The weather-wise of old times regarded Præsēpe with peculiar interest. When it was clearly visible they expected fine dry weather, while its gradual disappearance as the air thickened with moisture was regarded as a sign of approaching rain. On the whole, however, I think our modern Weather Probabilities more trustworthy than this and similar prognostics.

Next month, Hydra (the Sea-serpent) will have come fairly above the southern horizon, and will deservedly claim our attention.

In the east (p.82) the constellation of the Lion has passed much higher than last month, and is making room for Virgo (the Virgin). It will be observed that although in the eastern map nearly the whole of Virgo is shown, yet in the latitude of London only half of this constellation can be seen at the hours named under the map. Nor can much more be seen in any of the latitudes for which these maps are constructed. For if you take any of the horizon lines from that for New Orleans to that for London, you will find that a large part of the constellation lies below the horizon line so taken.

In fact it so chances that in the eastern skies for this month, at the hours named, there is no large constellation which either has not been already described or will not be

---

* This description is truer for European than for American nights, for the pleasant nights of spring come later in America than with us.

more suitably described hereafter. Next month Virgo will be fully above all the horizons of our maps. Boötes, which is now passing into view in the east, not from above the eastern horizon you will observe, but from the north-east ascending on a slant, will be best placed for observation in the east two months from now. The Great Bear, half of which can be seen high up on the northern side of our eastern map, does not in reality belong to the eastern or western sky views at all.

Thus the only eastern constellations which really require description this month are the small ones, Canes Venatici (the Hunting Dogs); Coma Berenices (the Hair of Queen Berenice); and Leo Minor (the Lesser Lion).

The Lesser Lion is one of Hevelius's absurd constellations. It occupies a space between the Great Bear and the Lion which might have quite readily been divided between these constellations. I believe the small stars forming this constellation originally marked the mane of the Lion.

The constellation Coma Berenices, originally the tail of the Lion, is interesting to astronomers, because it must be regarded as a group of stars really forming a system. It is quite incredible that if the stars in space were really scattered independently of all relation to each other, such groups as the Pleiads or Coma Berenices would be formed by the apparent concourse of stars really lying at very different distances but seen accidentally (so to speak) in the same direction. Although Coma (as this constellation is now conveniently named by astronomers) is not nearly so closely set a group as the Pleiads, the reasoning which obliges astronomers to regard the Pleiads as a real cluster of stars, can be applied with equal force to Coma Berenices. It is simply a more diffuse cluster. The story of the constellation is interesting, but apocryphal. It runs that Berenice vowed to offer her hair to Venus if her husband, Ptolemy Euergetes, should be victorious over his enemies. On his return in triumph, he was pained to find her closely shorn; and to comfort him they sent for the priests and astronomers, who found somehow that the queen's hair had been placed among the stars. Modern astronomers are not equal to feats of this kind.

There is very little to be said about Canes Venatici, or "the Hunting Dogs." The constellation was invented by Hevelius, according to his usual fashion of filling in spaces with new figures. It could have very readily been dispensed with. In this constellation lies the marvellous Whirlpool Nebula, which Whewell has (worthily) chosen as the subject for the frontispiece of his book on the plurality of worlds.

Turning to the west (p. 83), we find that Auriga (the Charioteer), which in January was on the eastern side of the point overhead, and last month was overhead, is now on the western side of that point. Gemini (the Twins) have come

Fig. 15.—Cepheus.

over from the south-east, where they were in January, to the south-west. It will be seen that our western maps will hereafter need very little description, since nearly all the stars which are seen at any time towards the west, were towards the east a few months earlier. The western maps, however, are very necessary. For though there is nothing new to be said (for instance) this month about the constellation Auriga, yet the aspect of this constellation when on the western side of the point overhead, is altogether different from that which it presented when on the eastern side of that point. So again, the eastern and western maps for *different* hours are necessary, because, owing to the slant motion of the stars across the eastern and western skies, the star groups change markedly in aspect from hour to hour.

I shall reserve to the month after next, the description of Orion's approach towards his

". . . grave, low down in the west."

# STAR MAPS FOR MARCH.

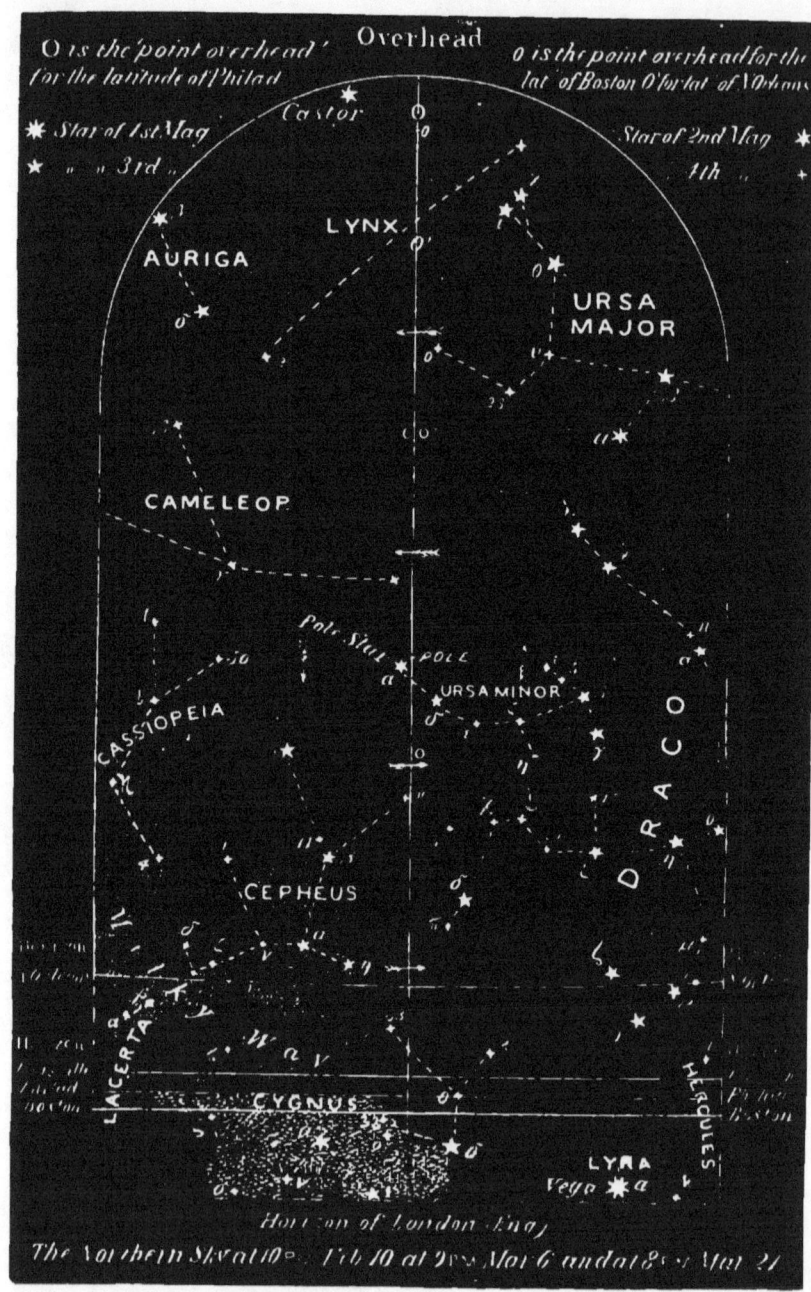

THE NORTHERN MAP FOR MARCH.

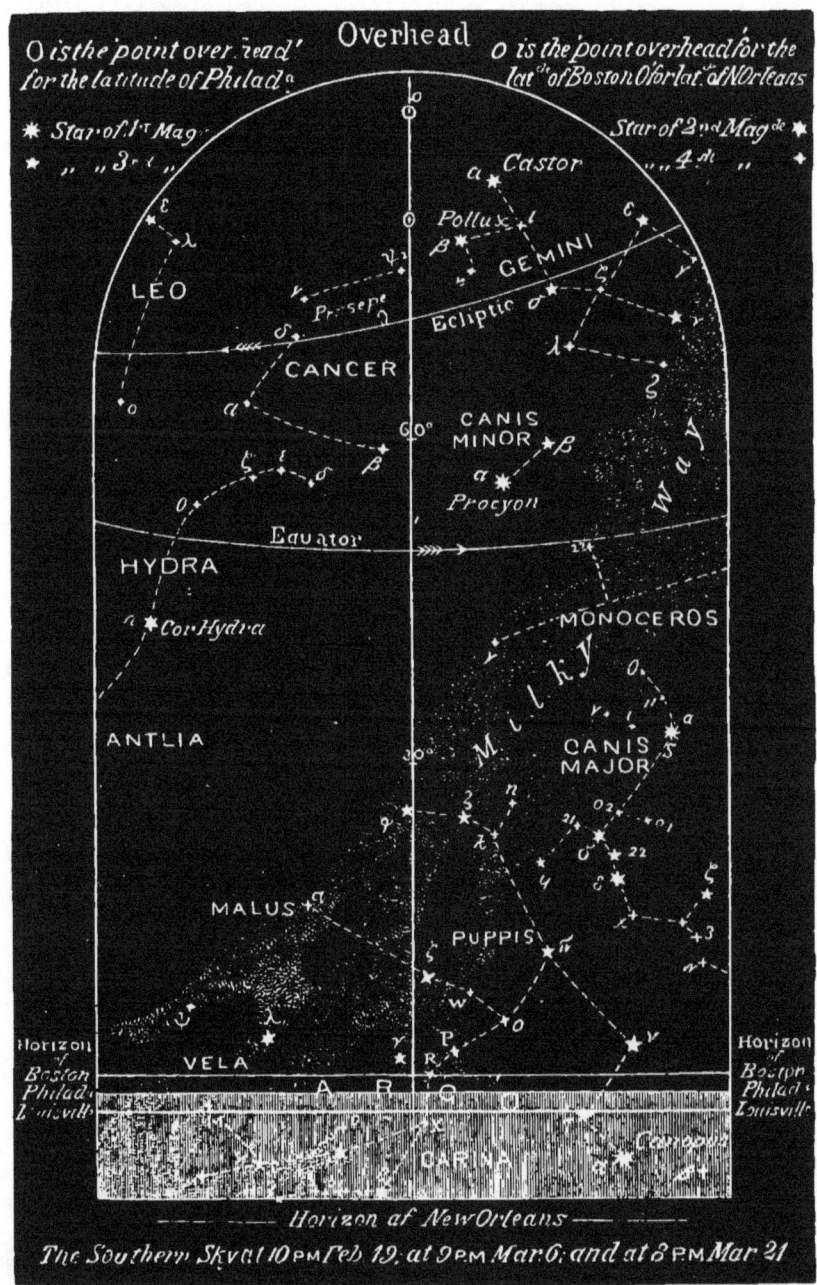

**THE SOUTHERN MAP FOR MARCH.**

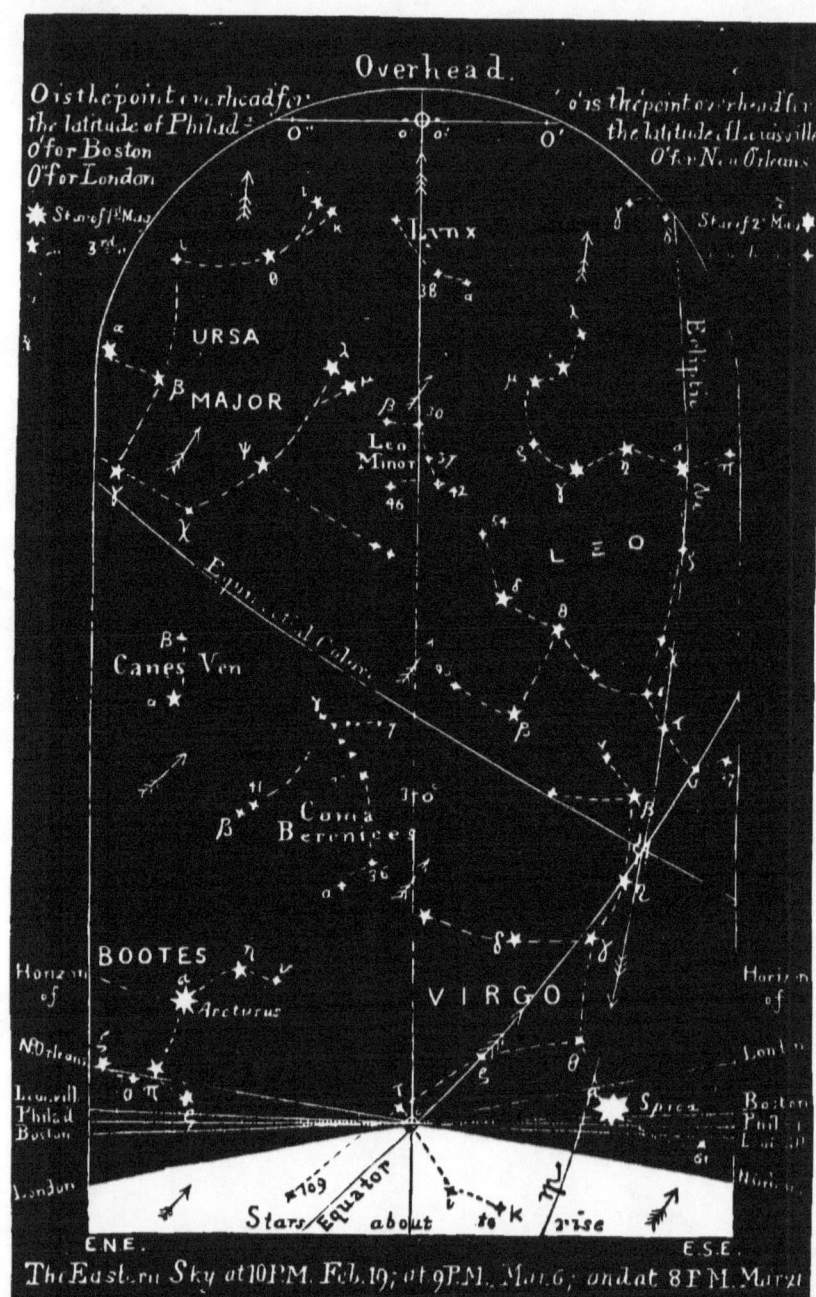

THE EASTERN MAP FOR MARCH.

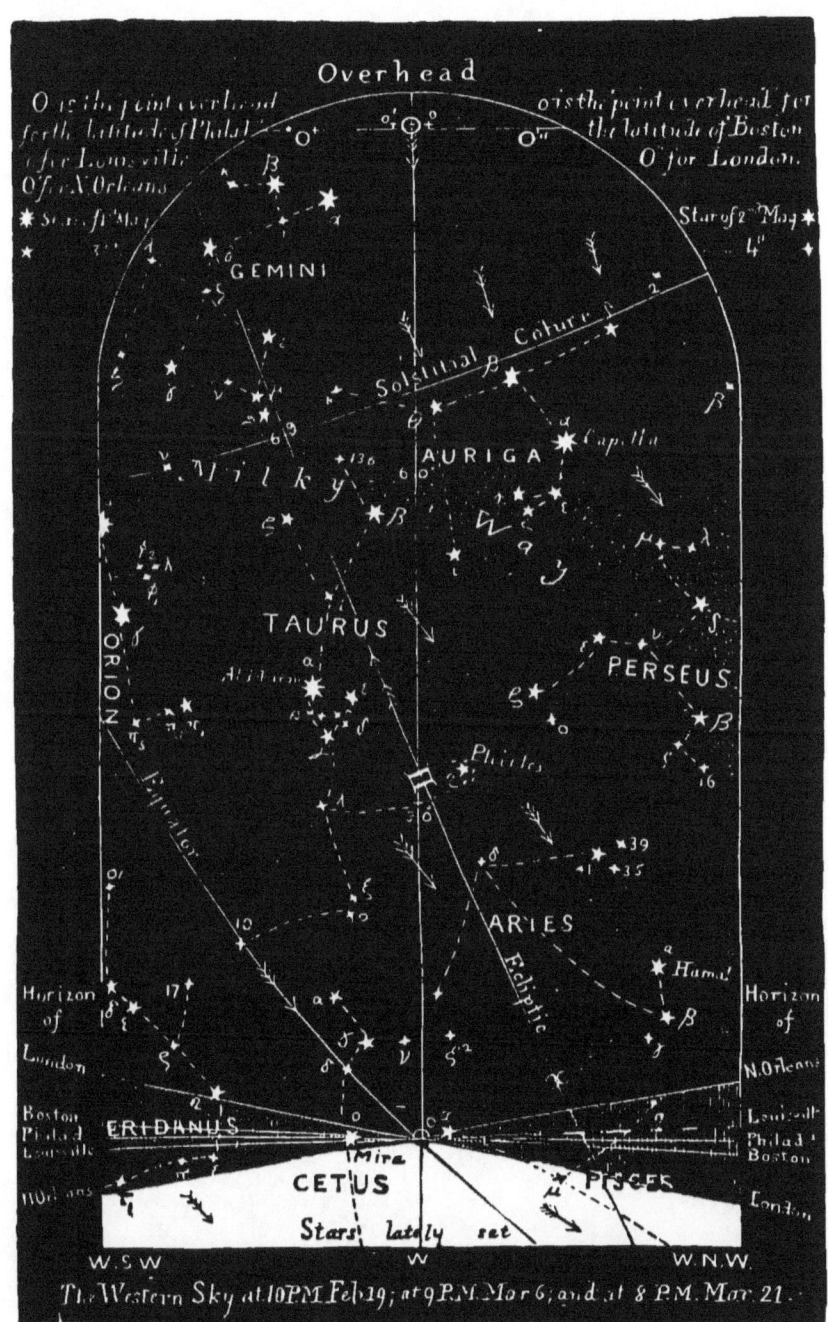

**THE** WESTERN MAP FOR MARCH.

# THE STARS FOR APRIL.

In the northern heavens (p. 98) we now see the Little Bear passing above the horizontal position which he had not quite reached last month. The Great Bear is now overhead, but inverted. The triplets of stars, $\psi$, $\mu$, $\lambda$ and $\theta$, $\iota$, $\kappa$ represent his paws, and I fear there is nothing better for his head than the small group $\upsilon$, $\theta$, and 23. The dreary constellation Lynx occupies the position shown  It was not one of the ancient constellations, but was invented by Hevelius, just as Camelopardalis (the Giraffe) was invented, to fill up a waste space in the star-charts. King Cepheus is now immediately below the pole, but still in unkingly attitude. The stars $\gamma$ and $\kappa$ represent his feet, flourishing wildly upward; $\zeta$, $\epsilon$, and $\delta$, as I mentioned last month, represent his head; and $\iota$ marks the place of his left hand, in which he bears a regal sceptre. Admiral Smyth, in whose "Bedford Cycle" there is much curious information about the constellations, gives the following doggrel account of the true position of Cepheus, according to Aratus and Ptolemy:

> "Near to his wife and daughter see,
> Aloft where Cepheus shines,
> That wife, the Little Bear, and Swan,
> With Draco, bound his lines;
> Beneath the Pole-star twelve degrees
> Two stars your eye will meet,—
> Gamma, the nomad shepherds' gem,
> And Kappa mark his feet.

> Alphirk (β), the Hindu's Kalpeny,
>   Points out the monarch's waist;
> While Alderamin (α), beaming bright,
>   Is on the shoulder placed;
> And where, o'er regions rich and vast,
>   The Milky Way is led,
> Three stars, of magnitude the fourth,
>   Adorn the Æthiop's head."

The story of Cepheus and his wife Cassiopeia, their daughter Andromeda, and Perseus, the gallant knight who rescued her from the sea monster (Cetus), does not belong to astronomy. But if it did, I should not venture to tell it here; for has it not been told already in Kingsley's charming poem "Andromeda?" How Perseus found means to gorgonize the sea monster with a petrifying stare is even more charmingly told in the "Tanglewood Tales," by the American prose-poet, Hawthorne.

Cassiopeia is following Cepheus, a little to the left, or west, of the north. You can always find Cassiopeia by noticing that it is almost exactly opposite the Plough, regarding the pole as a centre. Thus δ of the Great Bear, and α of Cassiopeia, are at the two ends, and the pole at the middle of a mighty arc on the heavens. Cassiopeia passes under the Pole-star in the same undignified position as her husband's. For you are not to suppose, as many (I find) do, that ε, δ, and γ form the back of Cassiopeia's chair, γ and κ the seat thereof, and ζ and β the ends of the chair's legs. These last are at ε and ψ, while ζ and β mark the place of the top rail. Still, in its present position, the group forms a very fair picture of a rocking-chair, θ, α, β, and 4 forming the rockers. Next month I shall speak more particularly about this constellation.

The portion of the Milky Way now under the pole is very irregular. In the constellation Cygnus you will see a great opening in the Milky Way. This opening is sometimes called the Northern Coalsack, though it is not nearly as black as the opening in the southern Milky Way near the Cross, which is the real Coalsack.

The region in which the Northern Coalsack lies is shown in the map of the northern sky. But a special map is added in Fig. 16, for another purpose. In 1876 a new star appeared in the constellation Cygnus (the Swan). On the evening of the 24th of November, Professor Schmidt, director of the Athens Observatory, noticed a star of the third magnitude at the place shown by the skeleton star in Fig. 16. Not only was no star of that brightness there before, or any star visible to the naked eye, but it was found when

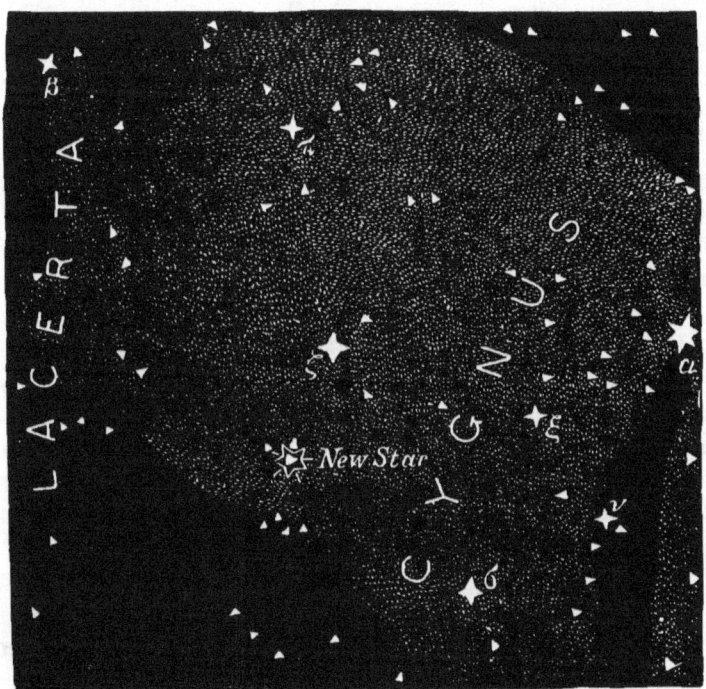

Fig. 16.—Part of Cygnus, showing where the new star of November, 1876, appeared.

catalogues and charts came to be examined, that no star had ever been noted there, even in lists meant to include all stars down to the tenth magnitude. For instance, Argelander has made such a list, and charts from it, showing no less than 324,000 stars,—that is, a hundred times as many as we can see on the darkest and clearest night; yet his list showed no star where the new one had appeared. Astronomers did not, however, infer that the new star is really new, except in the sense of being seen for the first time. They knew that when last a new star appeared in this way it was found to be one of Argelander's army of 324,000 stars, and watching that star (which had appeared in the constellation of the Northern Crown in May, 1866), they found that though it faded gradually out of sight to ordinary vision, the telescope could still follow it, until it had sunk to the tenth magnitude, at which degree of lustre it remained and still remains. Possibly if we had had full lists of all stars down to the fifteenth, or perhaps the twentieth, magnitude, we should have found that the new star in Cygnus was simply an old faint star which had brightened up suddenly, and remained for a time as one among the stars adorning our skies.

Examined with an instrument called the spectroscope the new star gave a very strange account of itself. It was found to be emitting the same sort of light as other stars; but besides that light, it emitted such light as comes from intensely heated vapours. Among the vapours in that star thus (for the time) intensely hot, were hydrogen, the vapours of the metals sodium and magnesium, and a vapour known to be present in enormous quantities in our sun's outer atmosphere, as seen during times of total eclipse. All these vapours surround our sun; and it is very probable that if anything caused our sun to blaze out with greatly increased light and heat, people living on a world circling round some other sun would find the same peculiarities in our sun's light as we have found in the light of the new star in the Swan. What caused that star to blaze out in that strange way we do not know. We should like to know, because we might then determine whether the cause which had so disturbed that sun might not be one from which our own sun may one day suffer. Whatever the cause was, its effects did not last very long. In a week the new star had sunk to the fifth magnitude, in another week to the sixth, in yet another to the seventh, since which time (December 15th) it has very slowly diminished, but on January 5th was still above the eighth magnitude. But later its light changed in character, in such a way as to show that the object was dying out into a mere mass of luminous mist, a nebula of the gaseous kind.

In the southern sky (p. 99), we find the great Sea Serpent, Hydra, occupying the leading position. This is the longest, and nearly the largest, of all the constellations. It is partly shown in our southern map for last month, and we shall not quite see the end of it for three months yet to come; so that it shows itself in no less than five of the southern maps. This is another constellation which has changed in position owing to the mighty reeling motion of our earth. When the constellation was first formed, the Sea Serpent extended along the equator; and I think originally represented the great serpent which was supposed to gird round the ocean. I have sometimes thought that when this constellation was framed (and Cetus, too), there may still have remained some few of those long-necked paddling sea-monsters whose skeletons are found from time to time in various parts of the earth. Mr. Gosse, in a sketch called the "Great Unknown," maintains that there are still a few of these monsters left, who being seen from time time to with their long necks reared above the sea, have been regarded as sea-serpents. And even though this may be unlikely or impossible, as Professor Owen seems to think, one may well believe that such monsters were either known or remembered, three or four thousand years ago.

The bright star Cor Hydræ or "the Serpent's Heart," is also called Alphard, or "the Solitary One." The head of the Sea Serpent is marked by the stars ζ, ε, and δ, which may be remembered conveniently, though absurdly, by the aid to the memory which I mentioned in the case of Cepheus's head last month.

The constellation Crater, or "the Cup," is a very neat one, and really like a rather damaged claret-cup. It is now tilted on one side, but formerly came to the south upright, as a well-filled cup should be. It has been regarded as the original goblet out of which Noah first took his wine, though since put to this higher use.

The ruling ecliptic constellation this month is the Lion (Fig. 17). You will know it at once by the magnificent

Fig. 17.—The constellation of the Lion.

sickle, formed of the stars α (Regulus or Cor Leonis, the Lion's Heart), η, γ, ζ, μ, ε, and χ. This group is sometimes conveniently called the Sickle in Leo. It is an interesting region of the sky for many reasons, but especially for this, that the wonderful shower of falling stars known as the November meteors, radiates always from this part of the heavens. The constellation of the Lion has been greatly reduced from its former noble dimensions. The figure shows how it is now presented in our charts; but if you look at the heavens, you will see nothing in the least degree resembling a lion. Still, if you allow your survey to range over a much larger space, you will see a very fine lion, his head lying on Cancer, his mane reaching to Leo Minor, his fore-paws on the Sea Serpent's head, his hinder paws on the two bright stars, shown in the figure (behind his hind-paws), which really belong to the Virgin, and his tail well represented by the constellation Coma Berenices, or Queen Berenice's Hair (shown in the figure, but not in the southern map). That this was formerly the real extent of the constellation, is shown by the fact that the star-cluster forming the chignon of Berenices is still called by Arabians the Lion's Tail; and there are vague traditions showing that Leo formerly extended to the constellation Gemini.

The Lesser Lion is one of Hevelius's absurd constellations. It occupies a space between the Great Bear and the Lion, which might have been divided quite readily between these two constellations. Sextans is another idle addition to the constellation figures. It is so called, apparently not because there are any stars, even small ones, forming a shape like a sextant, but because over a space not unlike a sextant there are none but very small stars.

Antlia, short for Antlia Pneumatica (the Air-pump), occupies another desert region. It was invented by Lacaille.

In the east (p. 102), the principal constellation is Bootes, the Herdsman. But though the stars of this constellation are now conveniently situated for observation, the constellation itself is not well placed. Bootes is figured as a man with uplifted arms; but, as at present situated, his figure is recumbent. In modern maps, one hand bears a club, the other holds the leash of the Hunting Dogs. Originally, however, the hands were probably empty. Certainly the right hand held no leash, for the constellation of the Hunting Dogs is a modern one. The description of Bootes may be conveniently deferred till August or September, when we shall have the Herdsman upright in the west.

The stars of the Serpent, shown underneath Bootes, form only one part of this constellation, which is divided into two separate portions on either side of Ophiuchus, or, as he is sometimes called, Serpentarius (the Serpent-Bearer).

It will be observed that the Greater Bear is passing up towards the point overhead, the stars of his impossible tail (the stars marked ϵ, ζ, and η in the map) travelling almost directly upwards. The "point overhead," or zenith, is now in this constellation at the times for which the maps are drawn, as will be seen by comparing the eastern and western maps for the present month.

In the west (p. 103), Taurus (the Bull) is passing away towards the right; Gemini, followed by Canis Minor (the Lesser Dog), is approaching the mid-west, or the prime vertical, as the great circle is called which is represented by the central vertical line in the maps, both eastern and western.

Orion is passing towards his setting-place in the west. Next month, at the hours for our maps, Orion will have almost wholly set, so that now is the proper time to describe this noble constellation,—at least, the proper time when a western view of Orion is to be considered. He really presents his noblest appearance when towards the south, where he was at the hours named in the maps for January and February.* But, as I have already mentioned, the student of the stars should know the constellations in all their principal aspects.

An hour or so later than the hours named under the maps, the aspect of the western skies will be that described by Tennyson in the beautiful lines quoted on p. 70.

It should, however, be noticed that Tennyson fails, as poets are apt to do, to indicate with precision the time either of the year or of the night which these astronomical relations are supposed to determine. The aspect described is presented at about ten in the evening on April 5th; but it is also presented at about nine on April 20th, at about eight on May 5th, and so on; as also at about eleven on March

---

* These vague expressions, as here, and when a few lines before I spoke of Bootes, are correct, because a constellation lies *towards* a given cardinal point at a given time for several weeks in succession. Of course, it would not be correct to say Orion lies *due* south at the times named above, still less to say that any given star so lies.

21st, at about midnight on March 6th, at about one in the morning on February 16th, and so forth.

For a description of Orion, the most beautiful constellation in the heavens, see p. 47.

The constellation Gemini, or the Twins, is now approaching the west, and occupies a different position from that which it had in our first map, when it was in the east though in both cases its distance from the horizon was about the same. When in the west the Twins were supine, now they are nearly in the attitude in which they are commonly represented in pictures of the constellation,—that is, in a half-reclining, half-sitting position. For a description of the constellation, the reader is referred to p. 29.

Auriga (the Charioteer) is perhaps as well placed for observation at this season as at any other throughout the year; but, to say the truth, the figure of the charioteer is never properly placed in our latitudes. The constellation passes overhead. When due north under the pole it is half concealed; when east or west at a convenient height for observation the charioteer is either falling backwards or is tumbling forwards. We must visit far higher latitudes than ours to see this constellation in the position in which it is figured in the books—that is, as a seated charioteer. He could be thus seen, when due south, at any station near enough to the north pole to throw Auriga considerably below the point overhead when he is crossing the meridian. At the time when the constellations were originally formed, the pole of the heavens was far removed from the present Pole-star, and Auriga was much farther from the Pole-star of that time. He was also differently posed, so to speak, and could be seen in the natural attitude of a charioteer when at a convenient distance above the horizon. I shall give hereafter a figure of this constellation. It is one of the forty-eight constellations of Ptolemy. The kids, or two stars $\epsilon$ and $\eta$, were for some reason regarded as stars of very evil portent, *horrida et insana sidera*—horrid mad stars. It was supposed that at their rising storms were certain to occur, nor does their approach to the western horizon seem to have been thought much more favourable. "Tempt not the winds," said Callimachus—

> "Forewarned of dangers nigh,
> When the Kids glitter in the western sky."

Capella, the chief brilliant of this constellation, is one of the brightest stars in the northern heavens. According to some astronomers this star shares with Arcturus and Vega the claim to be regarded as actually the brightest, though there can be no doubt that Arcturus surpasses both Capella and Vega in lustre.

# STAR MAPS FOR APRIL.

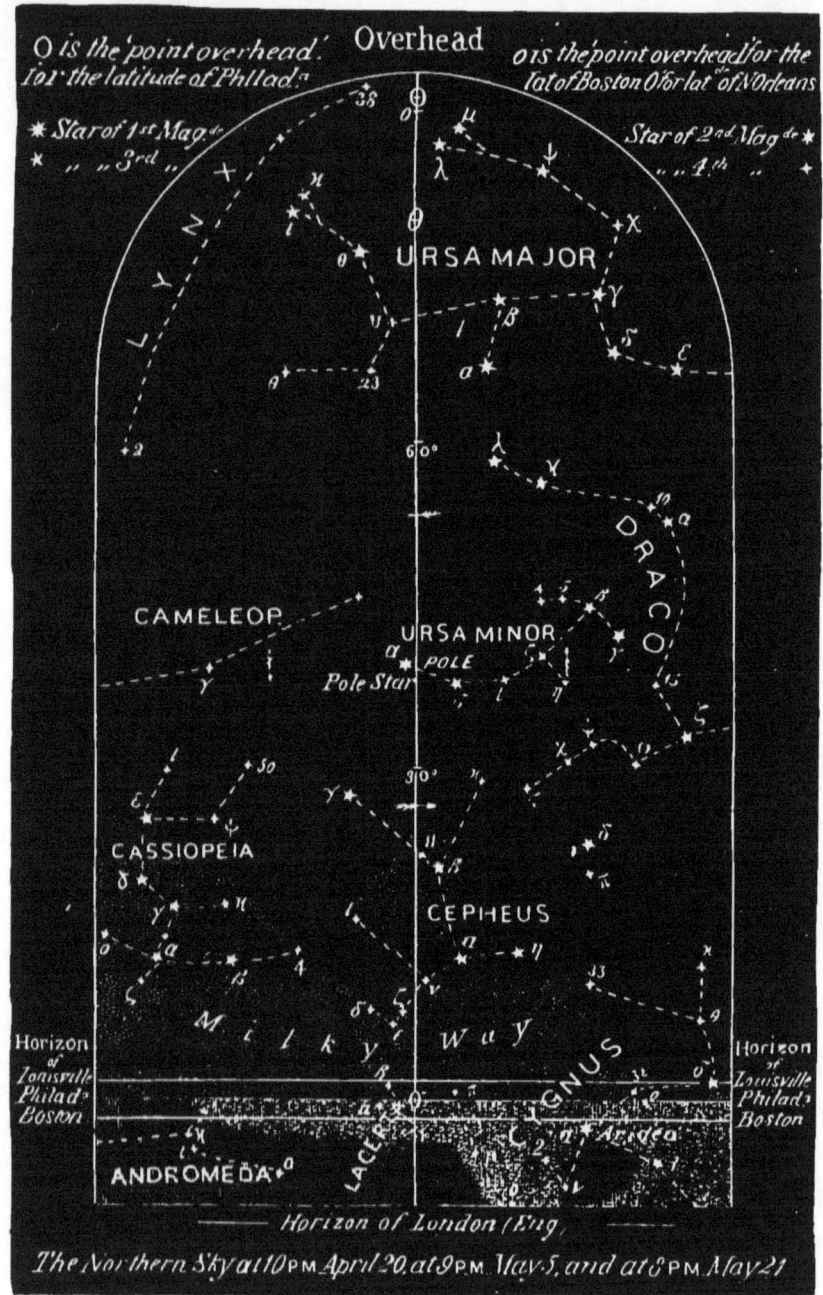

THE NORTHERN MAP FOR APRIL.

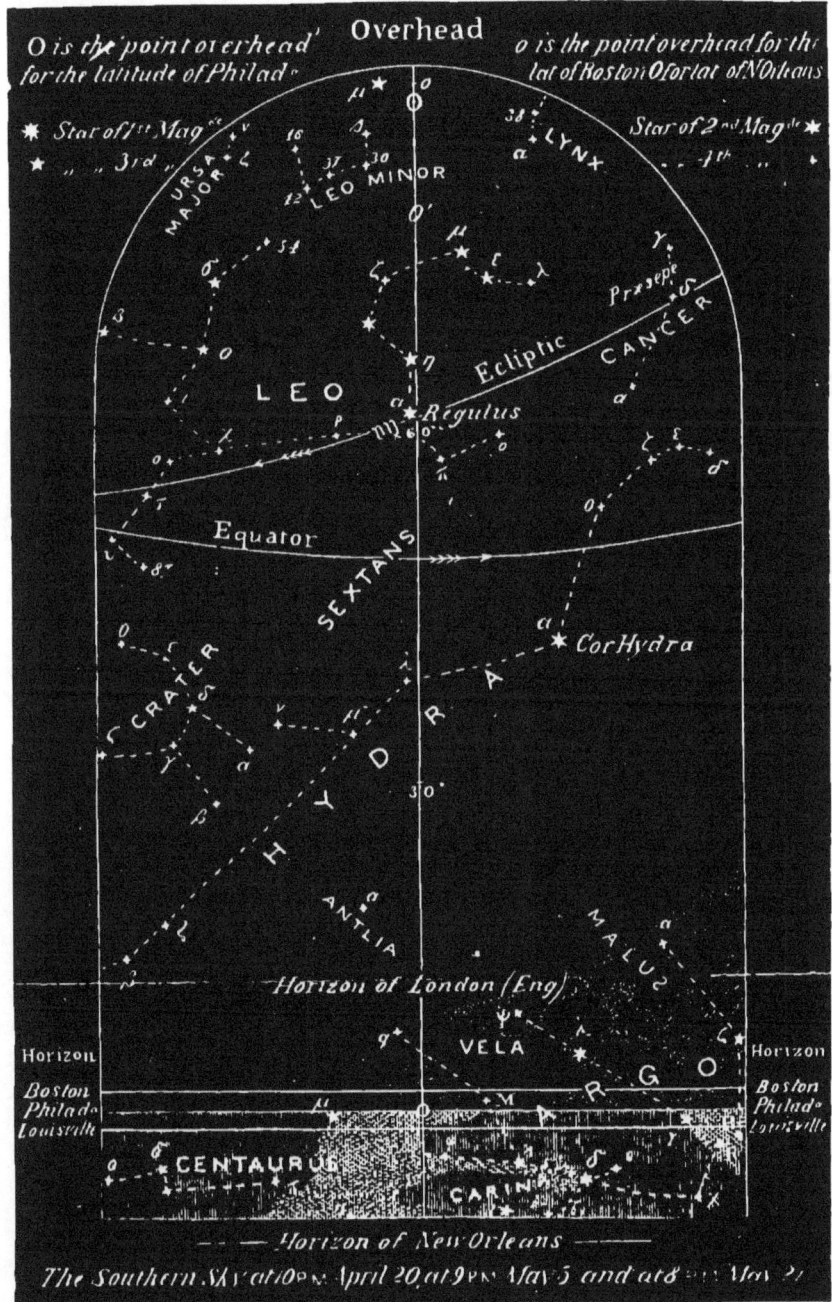

THE SOUTHERN MAP FOR APRIL.

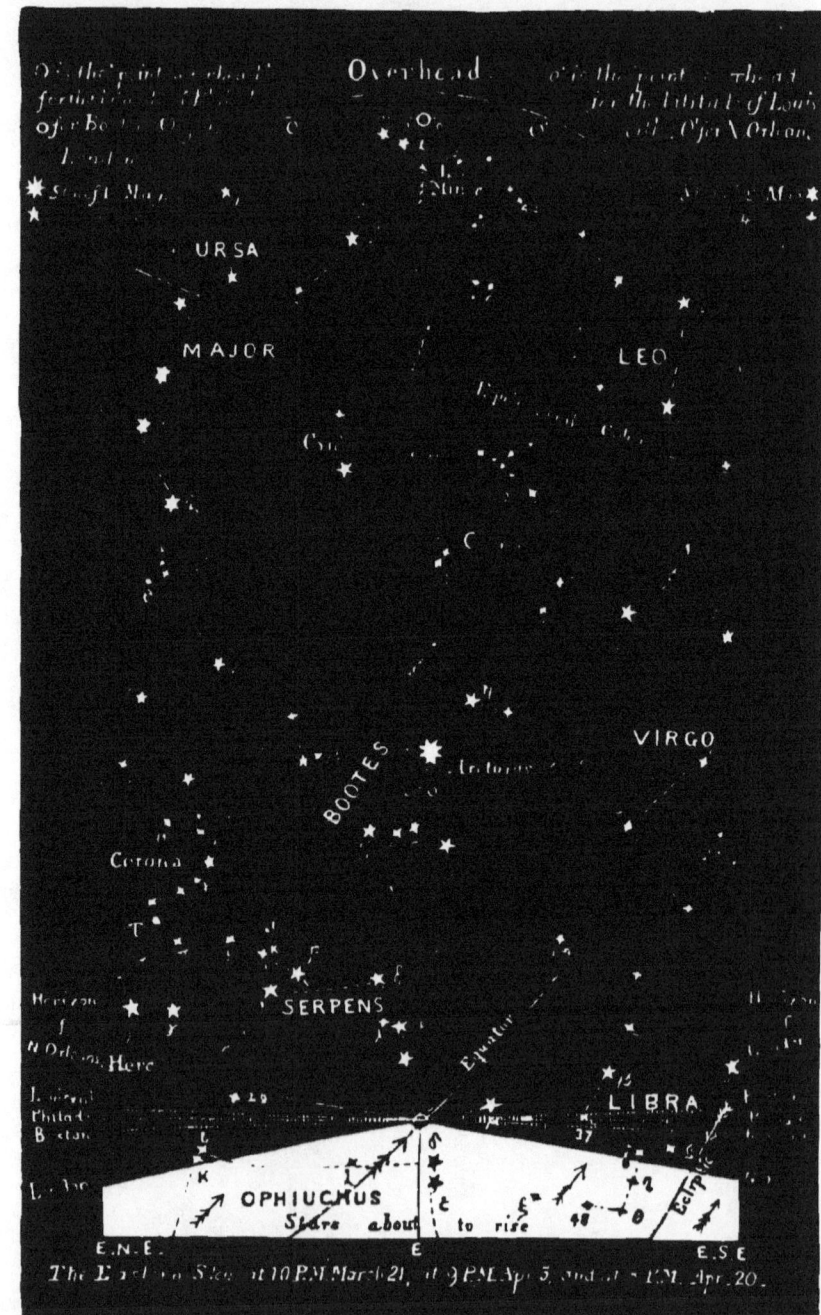

THE EASTERN MAP FOR APRIL.

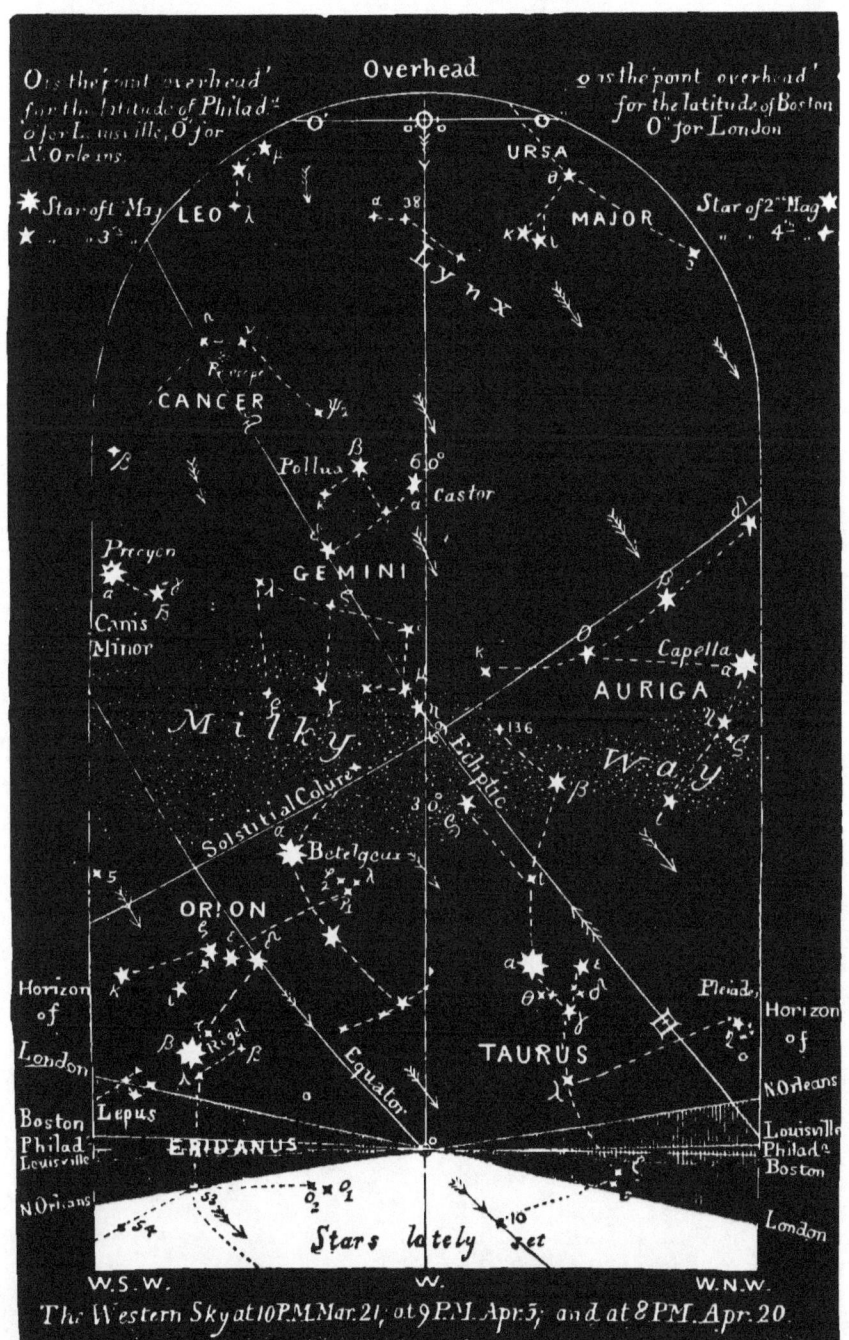

THE WESTERN MAP FOR APRIL.

# THE STARS FOR MAY.

TOWARD the north (p. 116), we now see the Plough, or Dipper raised directly above the Pole-star; the constellation of the Great Bear occupying a much wider region of the sky. The Little Bear, which last month had passed just above the horizontal position, has its length now in the position of the minute hand of a clock eight or nine minutes past the hour.

Since I wrote the account of the stars for April. I have come across a singular Arabian picture of a part of the northern heavens, from which it would seem that anciently the two Bears had their feet in the same direction. From the picture of the Little Bear, shown in Fig. 13, you will see that the feet of the animal are toward the stars $\eta$ and $\gamma$, or away from the Great Bear; and the feet of the Great Bear are toward $\mu$, $\lambda$, etc., of that constellation, or away from the Little Bear. So that the Bears are back to back;

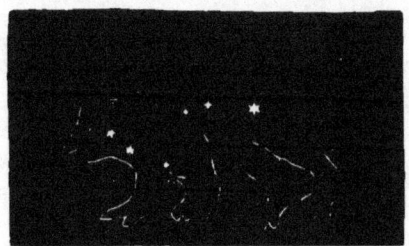

Fig. 18.—Ancient view of Ursa Minor.

and whenever one is placed, as in Nature, with his plantigrade feet lowermost, the other has his legs wildly waving above him,—which, on the whole, seems absurd. Now, in the old Arabian picture, drawn in the eleventh century, we find the Little Bear turned the other way. His tail still lies toward the Pole-star, but his feet lie toward the Great Bear, —the fore-feet at the stars 4 and 5; so that the Bears come into their natural attitude simultaneously. The accompanying picture (Fig. 18) is copied from the very rough drawing of the Arabian astronomers, except that the stars are represented a little more clearly than in their drawing. Only six stars are

Fig. 19. - Cassiopeia.

shown. The bear is not a very good-looking one, still he is more like a bear than the long-tailed creature in the account of the stars for March. To say the truth, astronomy cannot be said to distinguish itself pictorially, though serious confusion would follow a sudden changing of its familiar representations.

The constellation Cassiopeia (Fig. 19) is well placed in May for observation,—and I therefore give here a brief account of this ancient star-group.

According to Hyginus, Cassiopeia and Cepheus were placed in the heavens with their heads turned from the pole, so as to swing head downward beneath it, because Cassiopeia boasted that her beauty surpassed that of the Nereids. It is convenient to keep this in mind, not because her error of judgment (she had not even seen the Nereids) was of much importance, but as a help to the memory. The star $\zeta$, the remotest from the pole of all shown in our northern map as belonging to Cassiopeia, marks her head; and her queenly robes flow toward $\iota$ and 50, though in most pictures of Cassiopeia a raised dais is placed where these stars are. The figure shows the position of the lady with respect to the

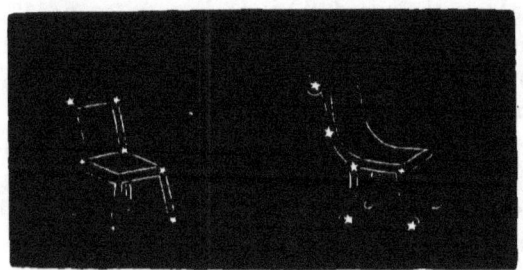

Fig. 20.—Two views of Cassiopeia's Chair.

stars. You will see that, in order to make it agree with the constellation as now seen, the picture must be inverted. Flammarion, in his book on the heavens, strangely mistakes the position of the chair. I quote from Mr. Blake's work based on Flammarion's, and for the most part a translation; but possibly the error is Mr. Blake's. He says "the chair is composed principally of five stars, of the third magnitude, arranged in the form of an M. A smaller star, of the fourth magnitude ($\kappa$), completes the square formed by the three, $\beta$, $\alpha$, and $\gamma$. The figure thus formed has a fair resemblance to a chair or throne, $\delta$ and $\epsilon$ forming the back; and hence the justification for its popular name." But, apart from the agreement of all the old authorities as to the position of the chair, there can be no doubt that the six leading stars of the constellation show a much closer resemblance to a chair, having $\beta$ and $a$ for the back, or like the first picture in Fig. 20; that, too, is the shape of ancient chairs. People who lived in the years B.C. did not loll; like Mrs. Wilfer in more recent times, they were "incapable of it." Now the group of stars placed as in the second drawing of Fig. 20 forms an unmistakably easy chair.

It is useful to remember the letters corresponding to the brighter stars, and any aid to the memory, however absurd in itself, is worth noticing if it helps to recall the arrangement of the letters. It will be observed that the five leading stars of Cassiopeia have the first five letters of the Greek alphabet. To remember their order, notice that, beginning with the top rail of the chair, they follow thus, $\beta$, $a$, $\gamma$, $\delta$, and $\epsilon$, making the word "bagde," or, *in sound*, "bagged." I have myself found this aid to the memory so often useful, that I do not hesitate to mention it, like those others relating to the heads of Cepheus and Hydra. (I add, in passing, that the head of Cassiopeia, like that of Cepheus, has a star $\zeta$ in it.) It is not with the least idea of raising a laugh about these absurd combinations that I mention them; though I can see no reason on earth why science should be studied always with a serious face. But these little helps to the memory, or others like them which the student can make for himself, are often very useful.

For instance, I proceed to note that the two stars $\gamma$ and $\epsilon$ of Cassiopeia point toward a most wonderful and beautiful cluster of stars, lying about twice as far from $\delta$ as $\delta$ does from $\gamma$. If you remember the names of the five leading stars, this direction at once shows you where to look for the cluster, without referring anew to any map. Of course, the northern map belonging to this paper also shows you how to find the cluster, which is marked in its proper place. But it is well to remember the way in which $\delta$ and $\gamma$ point to it. In the sky, the cluster can only just be seen on clear nights as a small round mist. If, however, you turn a small telescope, or even a good opera-glass, upon it, you will see that it is sparkling all over with stars. In a powerful telescope, it is one of the most wonderful objects you can imagine. You see at a single view, in that little spot of misty light, more stars—that is to say, more *suns*—than the unaided eye can see in the whole sky on the darkest and clearest night!

The constellation Perseus, or the Rescuer of Andromeda, is now approaching the region below the pole, and in England is fairly well seen when thus placed. But in the greater part of the United States, the southern half of the constellation passes below the horizon as it approaches the northern sky. It will be well, therefore, for American students to look for Perseus half an hour, or even an hour, earlier than the times mentioned in the northern Chart, noticing that the stars $\gamma$ and $\delta$—of Cassiopeia—or, better, the stars $\kappa$ and $\delta$—point toward Perseus. It is impossible to mistake the beautiful festoon of stars, $\eta$, $\gamma$, $a$, $\delta$, $\mu$, and $\lambda$, with other smaller stars shown in the northern map, which form the northern half of the constellation Perseus. In the section for June I shall give a brief account of the constellation, and especially of the star Algol, one of the most remarkable variable stars in the whole heavens.

For the present, however, we must turn toward the southern heavens, p. 117.

The zodiacal constellation for the month is Virgo, or the Virgin (Fig. 21). The maiden is usually represented as an angel, her head between the stars $o$ and $v$. and $\tau$ marking the upper part of the wing, while the other wing has its tip near $\epsilon$. She has in her hand an ear of corn, whose place is marked by the bright star, Spica, so that the young lady's feet lie on a part of the constellation beyond the range of the map. It is easy to recognize the constellation by the bright star Spica, and the corner formed by the five third magnitude stars, $\epsilon$, $\delta$, $\gamma$, $\eta$, and $\beta$. For some cause or other,—a celestial reason, no doubt, since no earthly reason can be imagined,—this corner was called by Arabian astronomers "the retreat of the howling dog." The order of these star letters is nearly identical with that of the five stars of the same magnitude in Cassiopeia—Begde instead of Bagde. According to the ancients, Virgo represented Ceres, or Isis,

Fig. 21.—Virgo.

or Erigone, or the Singing Sibyl, "or some one else," as Admiral Smyth conveniently adds; some of the moderns have recognized in her the Virgin Mary. Most probably she was at first intended to represent a gleaner in the field,

Virgo having originally been the constellation through which the sun passed in August, and Spica very near the place of the sun at gleaning time in the warmer parts of the temperate zone.

Above the Virgin is the pretty star-group called Coma Berenices, (often incorrectly called Coma Berenicis), or the Tresses of Queen Berenice. (See Fig. 17.)

Hydra's length still trails onward athwart the southern sky. The constellations Corvus (the Crow) and Crater (the Cup) are now well seen. A cup is rather strangely placed on a snake's back; yet you are not to suppose the cup belongs to the Virgin. The Crow is usually drawn as perched on the Snake, and pecking his back, the bird's head being where the stars $\epsilon$ and $a$ are shown. But it has always seemed to me that the little group reminds one more of a crow resting, with his head, as at $\eta$, depressed between the raised shoulders, whose top would be marked by the stars $\delta$ and $\gamma$. This bird has been claimed for Noah's raven.

The Centaur, or Man-horse, is moving toward the south; but will be better placed next month, when I will describe it. The Southern Cross shows about two-thirds of its height above the horizon of New Orleans, but its leading brilliant, the foot of the cross, cannot be seen from any part of the United States, nor any star of the Cross from the Northern States.

The parts of the heavens now in view toward the south, especially the Locks of Berenice and head and wings of Virgo, are very interesting regions for telescopic study, being crowded with little clouds of light called nebulæ, some of which are clustering collections of small stars, others formed of some kind of shining gas. We owe the discovery of most of these to the two Herschels, Sir William and Sir John, father and son, each the greatest astronomer of his day and generation.

The sun's path through Virgo carries him, as you see by the maps, descendingly across the equator. When he is at the place marked ♎, the sign for Libra, or "the Balance," the days and nights are equal. This is at the time called the autumnal equinox. The zodiacal constellations now to follow are those below, or south of the celestial equator.

In the east (p. 120), the constellation Bootes, or "the Herdsman," has passed high above its position last month, which is now occupied by the constellation Hercules, or "the Kneeler." Hercules is not now in the proper attitude of a kneeling person. For the star $a$ marks the place of his head, so that his feet are flourishing upwards. In fact Hercules never is seen in our latitudes as a kneeling man. When he is at a convenient height for observation in the west, he is supine, while now in the east he is nearly prone, as one who has fallen almost headlong, and face downwards, from a height. Due east, and just above the horizon, is Ophiuchus (the Serpent-holder), supposed by some fanciful persons to have been typical of the Messiah. Although the part of the serpent shown on the white ground below is not visible in the northern latitudes, for which the maps are made, and even the stars $\nu$ and $o$ are not visible in London, it will be well for the student to notice that the other part of the Serpent, now conspicuous at a fair elevation between the east and east-north-east, does not form the whole of that constellation, which is perplexingly intertwined with the Serpent-holder.

Very little need be said about the western map (p. 121), as all the constellations which appear in it have already been described. The student will observe, however, how well situated the constellation Gemini is for observation at the times named under the maps. The twin stars, Castor and Pollux, are nearly at the same level, and the figures of the Twins may now be conceived as nearly upright.

# STAR MAPS FOR MAY

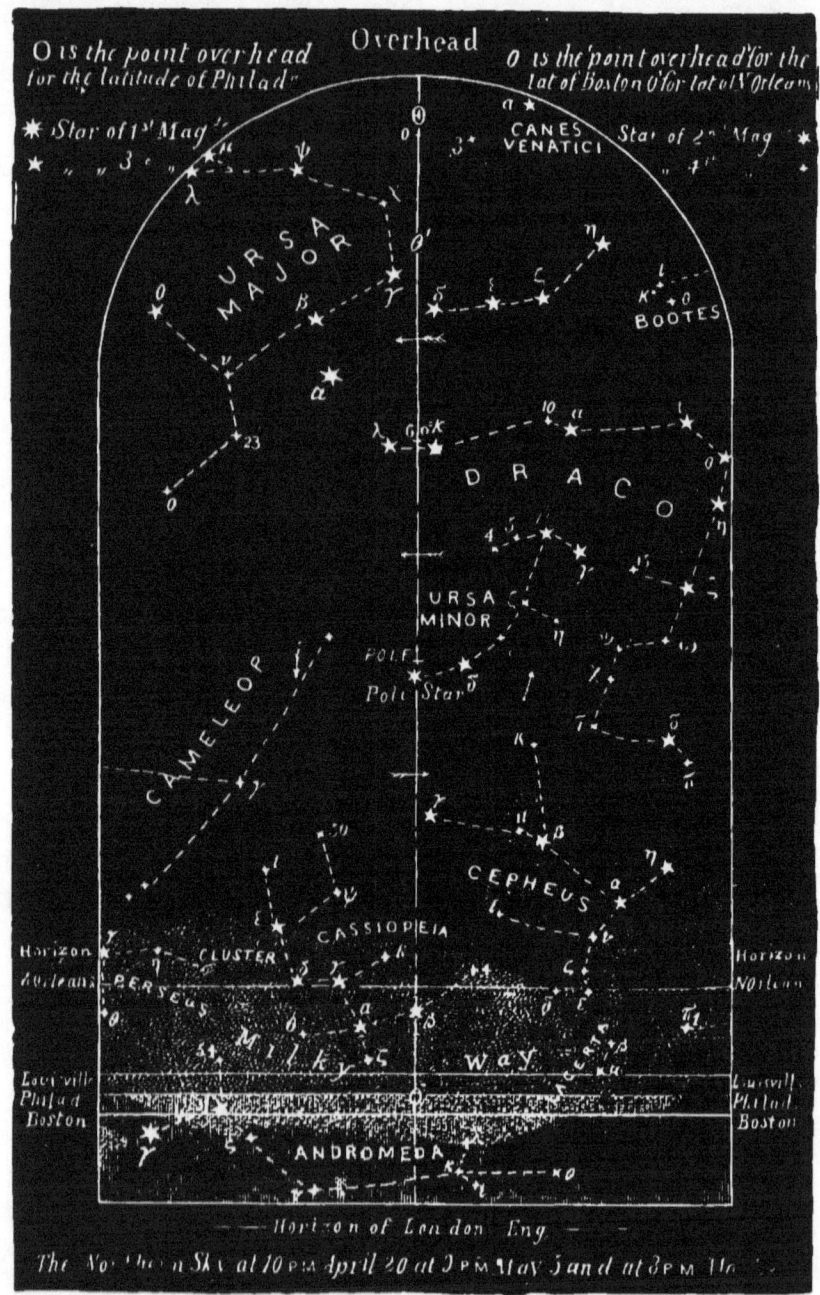

THE NORTHERN MAP FOR MAY.

117

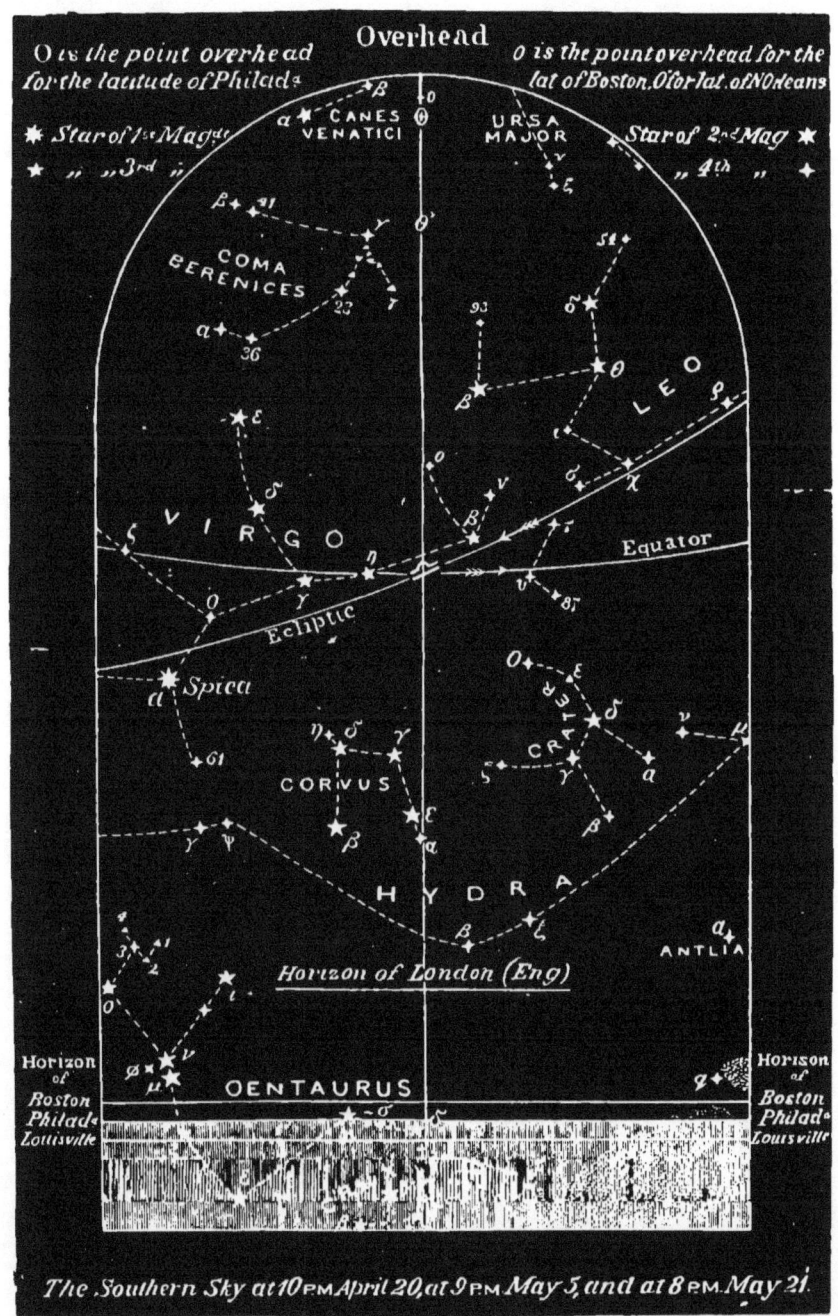

THE SOUTHERN MAP FOR MAY.

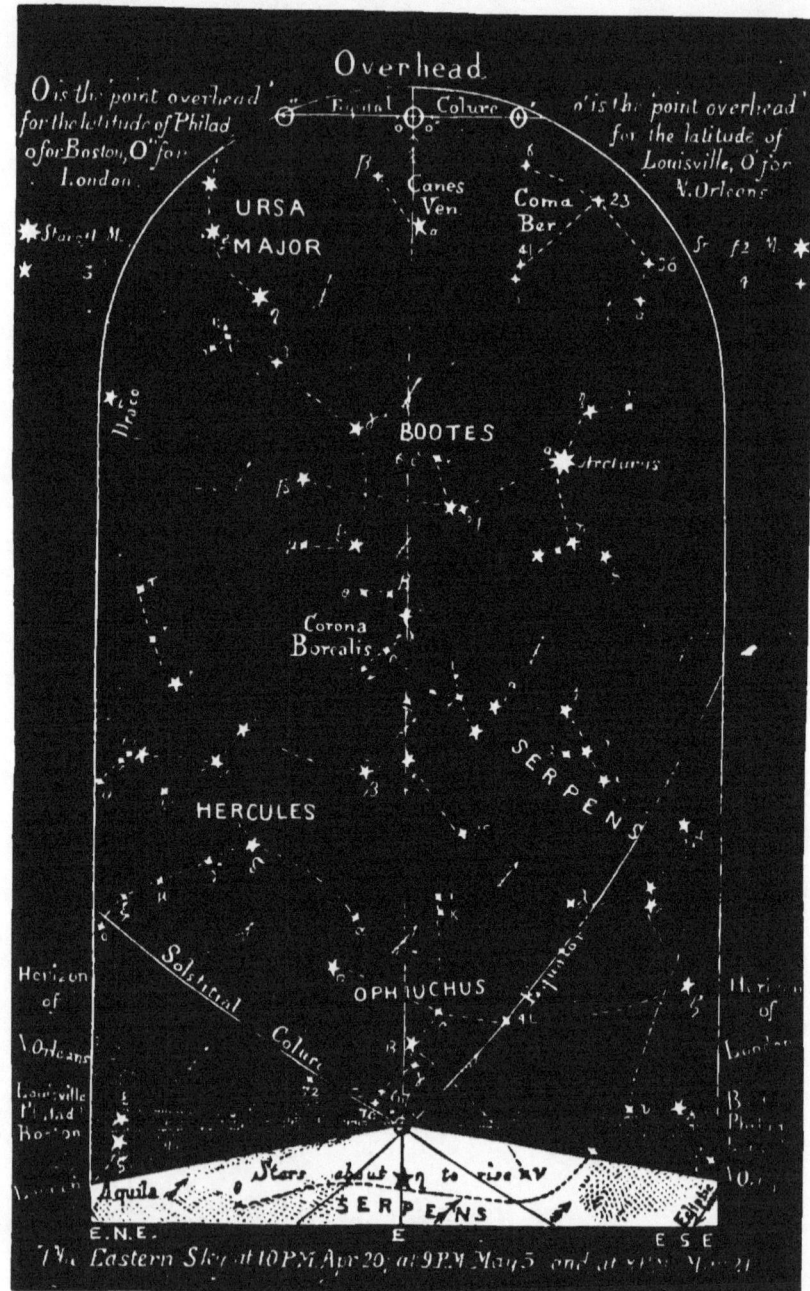

THE EASTERN MAP FOR MAY.

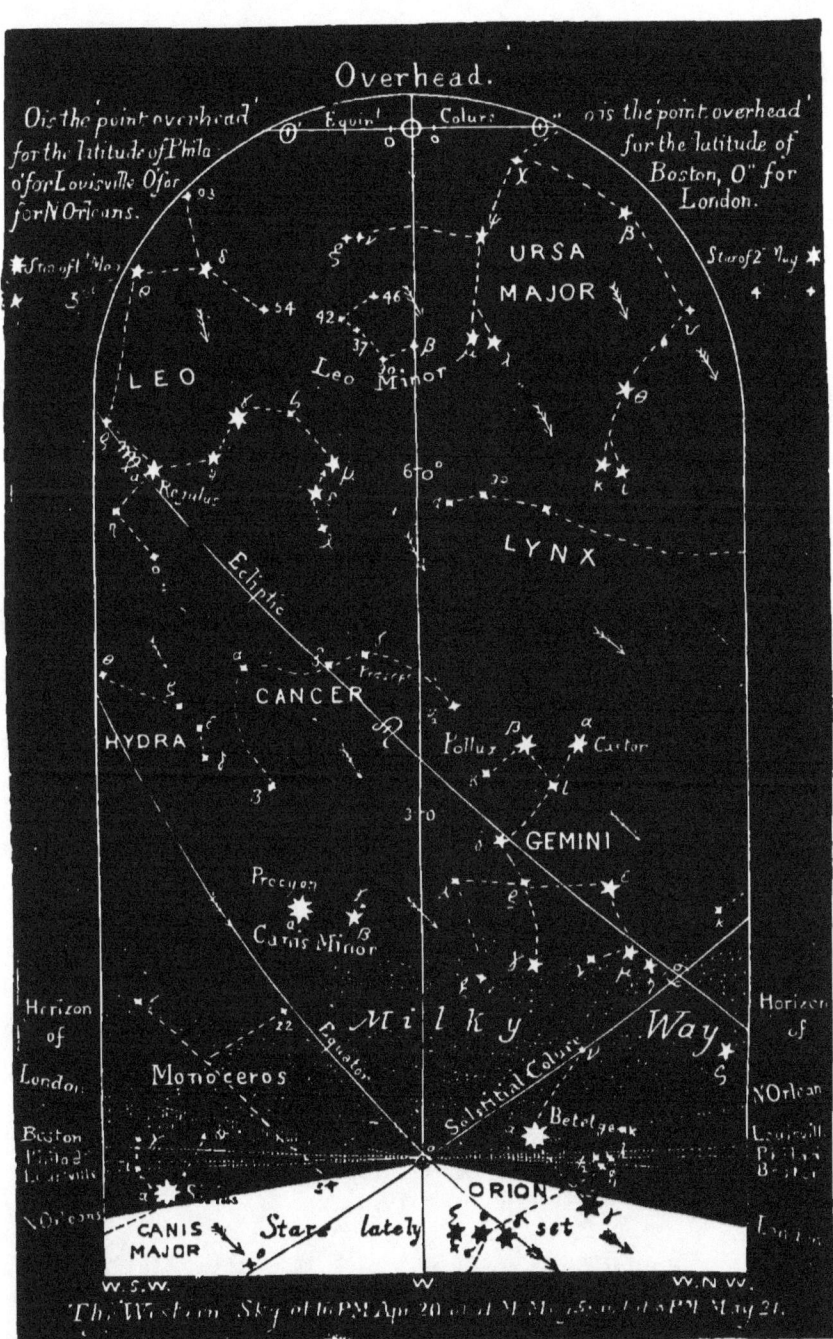

**THE WESTERN MAP FOR MAY.**

# THE STARS FOR JUNE.

This month, it will be well for the student to use the maps given for next month, because the evenings are now getting long, and the stars must be looked for later. Thus, the northern or southern map for this month shows the stars as they are seen on June 21st at eight; but at that hour it is not dark enough to see the stars. Now, the northern and southern maps for next month show the stars as they are seen on June 21st at ten o'clock. In July and August, also, it will be well to use maps of the stars at later hours than eight or nine.

In the northern map (p. 134) we find the Guardians nearly above the pole. The Plough, or Dipper, has passed to the left, or west, of due north. The last star of the Great Bear's tail is nearly overhead. Cassiopeia has passed below the pole toward the east, and the five bright stars of the constellation now make a straggling W close to the horizon, and very nearly upright. The festoon of stars belonging to the constellation Perseus is just visible above the latitude of Philadelphia, but better seen above the latitude of Boston. As far south as Louisville, the festoon at the hours named under the map is broken by the horizon; but half an hour earlier can be well seen. In London, as shown by the map, we can see at these hours nearly the whole of Perseus; and also a large part of Andromeda,—a constellation which cannot be well seen within the range of our northern maps from any part of the United States.

The constellation Perseus is one of the oldest. It belongs,

with Cepheus, Cassiopeia, Andromeda, and Cetus (the Sea Monster), to a set which has been called the Cassiopeian group,—illustrating the story of the pride of Cassiopeia. I have already referred to the story itself, as not belonging to our subject here. But how the story found its way into the heavens is one of the most mysterious questions in the history of astronomy; and if the answer could be found, we should have made an important step toward determining what nation first studied the stars. A curious story is told by Wilford, in his Asiatic researches, about these constellations. Asking an Indian astronomer, he says, "to show me in the heavens the constellation Antarmada," he immediately pointed to Andromeda, though I had not given him any information about it beforehand. He afterwards brought me a very rare and curious work in Sanscrit, which contained a chapter devoted to "*Upanachatras*," or constellations not in the zodiac, "with drawings of *Capuja* (Cepheus) and of *Casyapi* (Cassiopeia) seated and holding a lotus-flower in her hand, of *Antarmada* chained, with the fish beside her, and last, of *Parasica* (Perseus), who, according to the explanation of the book, held the head of a monster which he had slain in combat; blood was dropping from it, and for hair it had snakes." But whether the Indians borrowed from the Greeks, or the Greeks from the Indians, or both from some other source, we do not know.

Perseus is represented as in Fig. 22. Why, instead of a sword, the Rescuer should carry a weapon which looks like a reaping-hook, this deponent sayeth not,—not knowing. Admiral Smyth remarks, that in an ancient MS. of the astronomical poet Aratus in the British Museum, with drawings made, it is supposed, in the reign of Constantine, Perseus is represented with no other drapery than a light scarf, holding the head of Medusa in his left hand and a singular hooked and pointed weapon in the right. In the Middle Ages, an earnest effort was made to dismiss Perseus and Medusa's head in favour of David with the head of Goliath, but the attempt failed.

The cluster on the sword hand of Perseus (see the northern map, also) can be seen easily with the naked eye. This cluster should be examined with a small telescope, by all who possess, or can beg or borrow one. Nothing more wonderful exists in the heavens than this splendid cluster. In the middle there is a beautiful coronet of small stars.

Although Algol, in the head of Medusa, cannot be seen in America where shown,—the horizon of Boston passing high above it,—yet as its place will soon be learned when once the festoon of stars in Perseus ($\mu$, $\delta$, $a$, $\gamma$, and $\eta$) is known, I may take this opportunity of describing this remarkable star. It shines most of the time as a star of the third magnitude. During two days, fourteen hours, it retains this brightness; then, in the course of three hours and a quarter, it is reduced to the fourth magnitude. It remains thus faint for about a quarter of an hour, and then in the course of three hours and a quarter it gradually recovers its usual lustre. This regular change is accounted for by some astronomers 'by supposing the body of the star to rotate on an axis, having part of its surface not luminous." It is singular that Sir W. Herschel and others who have given this explanation should not have noticed how it fails when put to the test. The star loses half its brightness for about a quarter of an hour, out of sixty-nine hours, and remains in all only six hours and three-quarters below its full brightness. Now, if one side or part of a sun were less bright than the rest, to such a degree that, when that side was looked at, the sun shone with only half the lustre of its other side, then the sun would be certainly quite half the time below its full brightness, and probably longer. Try the experiment with an orange. Peel off so much of one side that when you look at that side about half is peeled and the other half unpeeled, and suppose the unpeeled part of the orange made intensely bright and and the peeled part dark. Now, let the orange spin steadily on an axis, either thrusting a stick through it, or hanging by a thread. You will find the peeled part remains wholly in view for (roughly) about a third part of an entire turning, and partly in view nearly twice as long. This is very unlike what is observed in the case of Algol, whose dark part, on the theory we are considering, would remain wholly in view only about a three-hundredth part of an entire turning, and more or less in view only about a tenth part. This could never happen. The only possible explanation seems to be this,—that there is a great dark orb, like our earth, only very much larger, travelling round that distant sun, once in about sixty-nine hours, and coming between that sun and us once in each circuit. It must be large enough to cut off about half that sun's light, and

Fig. 22.—Perseus the Rescuer.

must travel at such a rate that the partial eclipses which it causes last nearly seven hours at a time from beginning to end.

The discovery that Algol changes in brightness in this strange way is commonly supposed to belong to late times, but I think the name of the star shows that the astronomers of old knew all about this star's changes of lustre. You see from Fig. 22 how the star adorns the head of the Gorgon Medusa, borne by Perseus, which was supposed to possess the power of turning to stone every living creature that looked upon it. The Arabian name Algol is the same as *Al-ghûl*, the monster or demon. And to this star most evil influences were attributed by astrologers. All this seems to show that the old astronomers had found out how ominously the star looks upon our system, slowly winking upon us from out the depths of space.

Turning to the southern skies (p. 135) we find Virgo (the Virgin) now the ruling zodiacal constellation. Last month, she shared the honour with Leo (the Lion). Both these constellations are larger than others of the twelve which form the zodiac—the two together, instead of covering about sixty degrees of the sun's path (one-sixth of his circuit), covering fully eighty degrees, or between a fourth part and a fifth part. The next two—the Scales and the Scorpion—together, scarcely cover forty degrees, instead of covering about thirty degrees, or a twelfth part of the zodiac, a-piece. Nothing need be added to what I said last month about Virgo, and her bright star Spica. Libra (the Scales) I shall speak about presently.

The fine constellation Boötes (the Herdsman) is seen above Virgo. He is too high, however, for his figure to be readily recognized. At New Orleans, indeed, and other places far south, about as much of his frame is on the northern as on the southern side of the point overhead. The bright star Arcturus is a very noted one. According to the measurement of its light by Sir J. Herschel, it is the brightest star north of the celestial equator, though to the unaided eye, Vega, in "the Lyre," and Capella, in "the Charioteer," seem equally conspicuous. The heat which reaches us from this star has been measured, and is found to be equal to about as much heat as would be received from a three-inch cube, full of boiling water, at a distance of 383 yards!

Low down toward the south you see the stars of the Centaur and Lupus (the Wolf). But it is only from the latitude of New Orleans that the bright stars marking the fore-feet of this constellation can be seen. The stars of the

Cross marked in former times the hind feet. You can easily see how the figure was imagined—the stars θ and ι marking the shoulders, and 1, 2, 3, and 4, the head, of the human part of the Centaur; while the back of the horse extended from ζ to γ, σ, and δ. He was represented as bearing the body of the wolf upon a spear, apparently by way of offering it as a suitable sacrifice upon the altar, Ara—a constellation which a little later comes into view in the southern sky in places as far south as New Orleans.

In the east (p. 138) the constellation Boötes, which at the same hours a month earlier had been high above the eastern horizon, has passed almost to the region overhead, the most conspicuous part of the constellation lying towards the south. Hercules has passed into the position occupied last month by Boötes. This constellation is still prone, as one who has fallen headlong and face downward from a height. Ophiuchus has passed away from the east, and in his place, but low down, is Aquila, the Eagle. The small but beautiful constellation Lyra, the Lyre, is approaching the east. The brilliant Vega shines with a tint decidedly different from that of Altair, the chief star of Aquila, Vega having a slightly bluish colour. Both differ still more markedly, however, from the orange-yellow Arcturus, now shining high in the southern skies.

The part of the Milky Way now risen into view in the east is worth examining. Two streams can be recognised, one however,—the uppermost,—comes to an end where it reaches the constellation Ophiuchus. It is singular, that this stream, which is thus lost from excessive faintness on the right, is much brighter on the left (I refer always to the part of the heavens included in the eastern map) than the lower; whereas the lower stream, which is faint on the left where it crosses Vulpecula and Sagitta, is very bright and conspicuous on the right where it crosses Aquila. I have attempted to explain this singular feature in my "Universe of Stars."

The constellation Aquila was formerly conjoined with

another called Antinous; but now Antinous has disappeared from our star-maps.

All the constellations visible in the west (p. 139) have been already described, and nothing need be said about them. The student should, however, carefully compare the map with the heavens, noting that the aspect of the constellations, as they are now seen in the west, is entirely changed from that which they had presented in the east.

# STAR MAPS FOR JUNE.

131

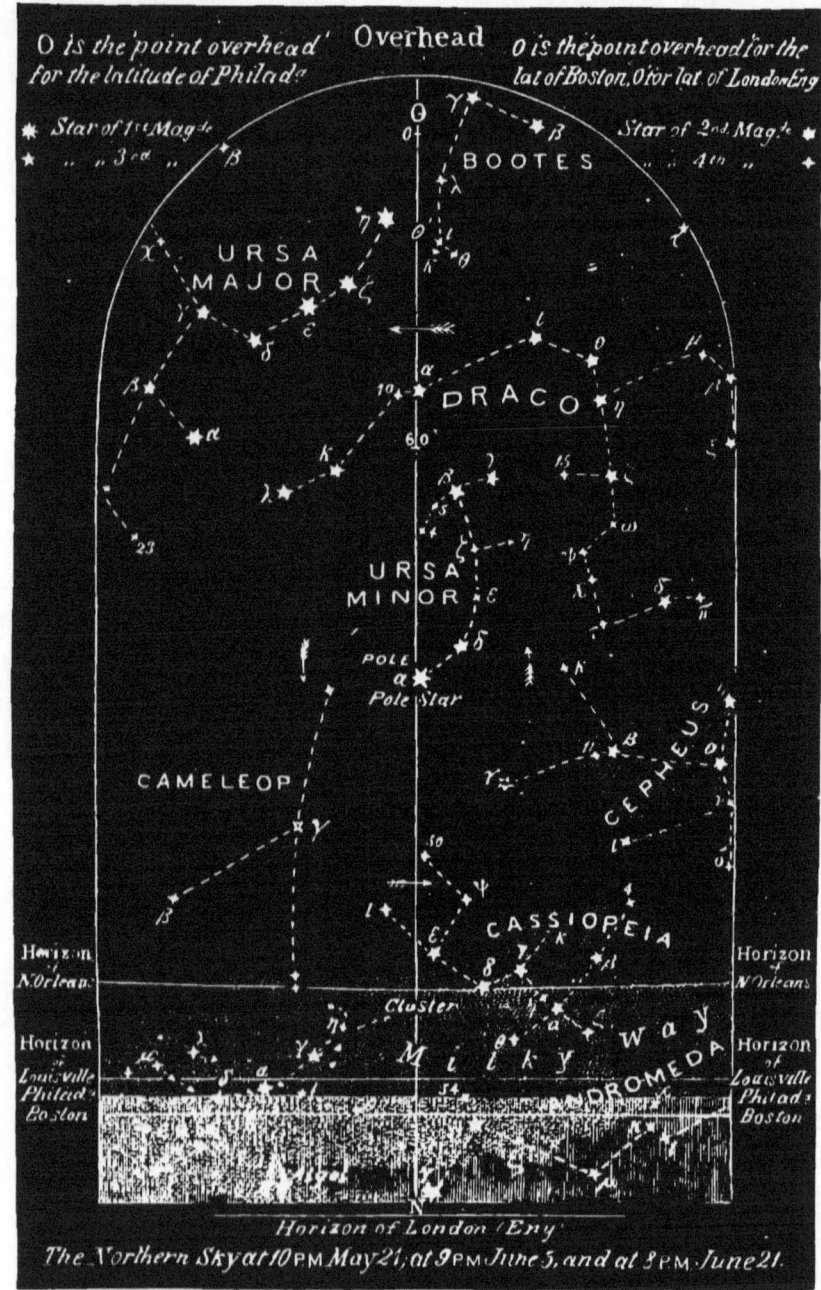

THE NORTHERN MAP FOR JUNE.

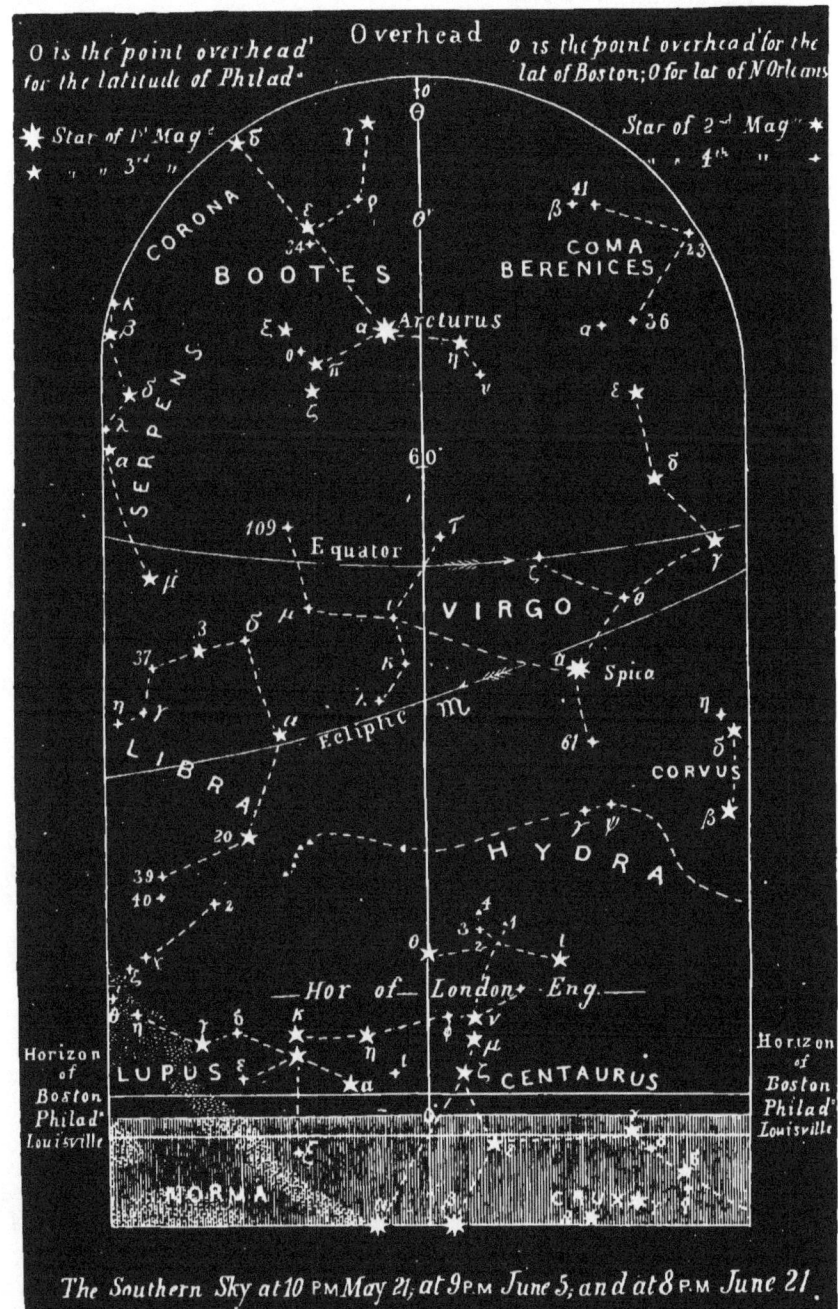

THE SOUTHERN MAP FOR JUNE.

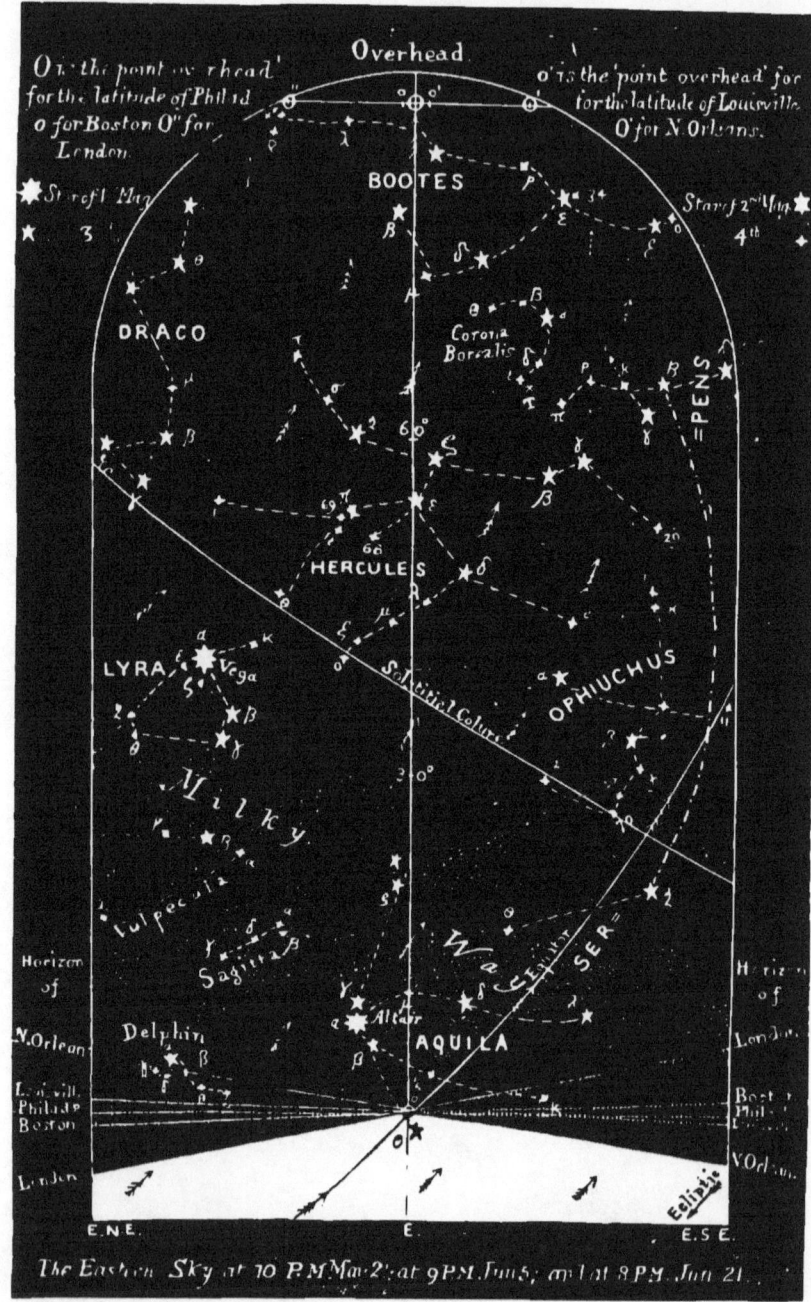

**THE EASTERN MAP FOR JUNE.**

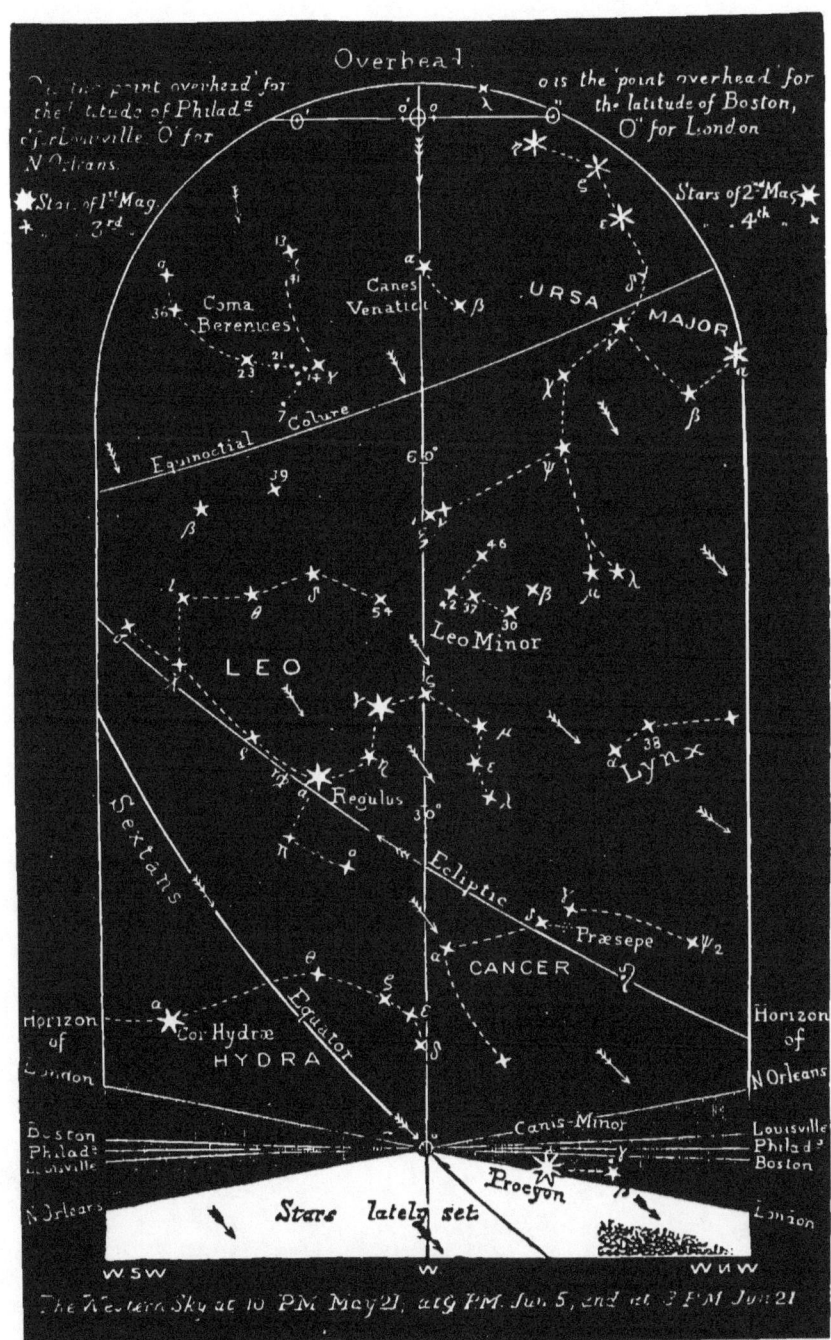

**THE WESTERN MAP FOR JUNE.**

# THE STARS FOR JULY.

In the northern map (p. 148) the Guardians have passed over to the left, or west, of due north. The Plough, or Dipper, now has its top—from $\delta$ to $a$—nearly perpendicular to the horizon. The Camelopard is below the pole. The solitary star marked 2, near the fore-foot of the Giraffe belongs to the Lynx, a constellation of small stars, set by Hevelius in this barren region of the heavens. The constellation Perseus has nearly passed from below the pole close by the horizon, and a part of Auriga is taking its place. But the bright star, Capella, which is the glory of this constellation, is beneath the horizon at the hours named below the second northern map, for all places south of the horizon of Boston, and even for two degrees or so north of that horizon.

It is toward the south (p. 149) that at present the heavens present the most glorious display. The contrast, in fact, between the northern and southern skies is very strange. Toward the north, the region below the pole shows not a single star above the fourth magnitude. Toward the south, the corresponding region (that is, the region extending some 40 degrees from the horizon) is singularly rich in large stars, chief among them being Antares (the Heart of the Scorpion), and perhaps the most beautiful of all the red stars. The word Antares means, in fact, "the rival of Mars." Antares cannot, however, really be said to rival, in ruddiness or in splendour, the planet of war when at his brightest.

Libra, which by rights should hold sway as the southern zodiacal constellation one month out of the twelve, has passed the south at the time shown in the southern map. The *sign* Libra has thirty degrees, like the rest, and pro-

Fig. 23.—Ophiuchus and Scorpio.

bably the original constellation had its due extension. A story is told by Servius to the effect that the original Chaldean zodiac had only eleven signs, and that Libra was made out of the claws of Scorpio. But there is ample evidence to show that both the sign and constellation Libra belonged to the earliest Chaldean and Egyptian zodiacs.

The figures of the Scorpion, Ophiuchus (the Serpent-bearer), with his serpent, besides parts of Hercules (head, arm and club), Libra (the Scales), Sagittarius (the Archer) and Lupus (the Wolf), are shown in Fig. 23.

The large constellation Ophiuchus is not specially interesting. It has been supposed by some to represent Æsculapius, and by others to be another celestial Hercules. Novidius insists that it prefigured the miracle of St. Paul and the viper, in which case the Maltese viper was considerably magnified in anticipation. The figure is a very absurd one, the legs being singularly feeble. But it must be admitted he is awkwardly placed. The serpent is quite enough to occupy his attention, yet a scorpion is ready to sting one leg and to pinch the other. The club of Hercules may be meant for the serpent, and the arrow of the Archer for the scorpion, but they seem to threaten the Serpent-bearer at least as much.

In the constellation Corona Borealis, a star marked T will be noticed. Here no star can be seen; but in May, 1866, one blazed out here very brightly, and, though it soon faded in lustre, it is still visible with a telescope. Like the star which blazed out lately in the constellation Cygnus, this one was found to be shining with the light of glowing hydrogen gas. At its brightest it appeared as a star of the second magnitude. Its present lustre is about one eight-hundredth part of that.

The ecliptic (the sun's path among the stars) still tends downward in both the southern maps. The place marked ♏ in the first southern map is that reached by the sun moving in the direction shown by the arrow on or about October 10, when, passing from the sign Libra, he enters the sign Scorpio, of which ♏ is the symbol. The place marked ♐ in the second southern map is that reached by the sun on or about November 22nd, when he enters the sign Sagittarius, of which ♐ is the symbol.

In the east (p. 152) the double part of the Milky Way has now risen high above the horizon, and in clear weather can be studied much more advantageously than a month later. The dark spaces, sometimes called the Northern Coalsacks, in the constellation Cygnus (the Swan), should be noticed. The whole of this part of the Milky Way is full of interest for the telescopist. Even with a good opera-glass, the bright parts of the galaxy here will be found to be ablaze with stars.

The little constellation Delphin, or Delphinus as it is more commonly called (but the shorter name is the better), is now conveniently situated nearly due east. Equus (more commonly called Equuleus), the Lesser Horse, is below it, Pegasus following from the left; but as both horses are upside down, the student of the stars must not expect to be very profoundly impressed by the resemblance between these groups and what they are supposed to represent— viz., Equus, a horse's head, and Pegasus, a winged half-horse.

The constellation Cygnus, or "the Swan," is now well placed for observation. The stars $a$, $\beta$, $\delta$, $\gamma$, and $\epsilon$, have been regarded as forming a cross, sometimes called the Northern Cross; and when the line $a$ to $\beta$ is upright, or nearly so, a cross may be very fairly pictured—a far finer cross, so far as size is concerned, than the famous Southern Cross. In the aspect presented on the map, however, the cross has its upright situated horizontally, or nearly so.

The same remarks may be made about the western stars for July (p. 153) as about those for June.

# STAR MAPS FOR JULY.

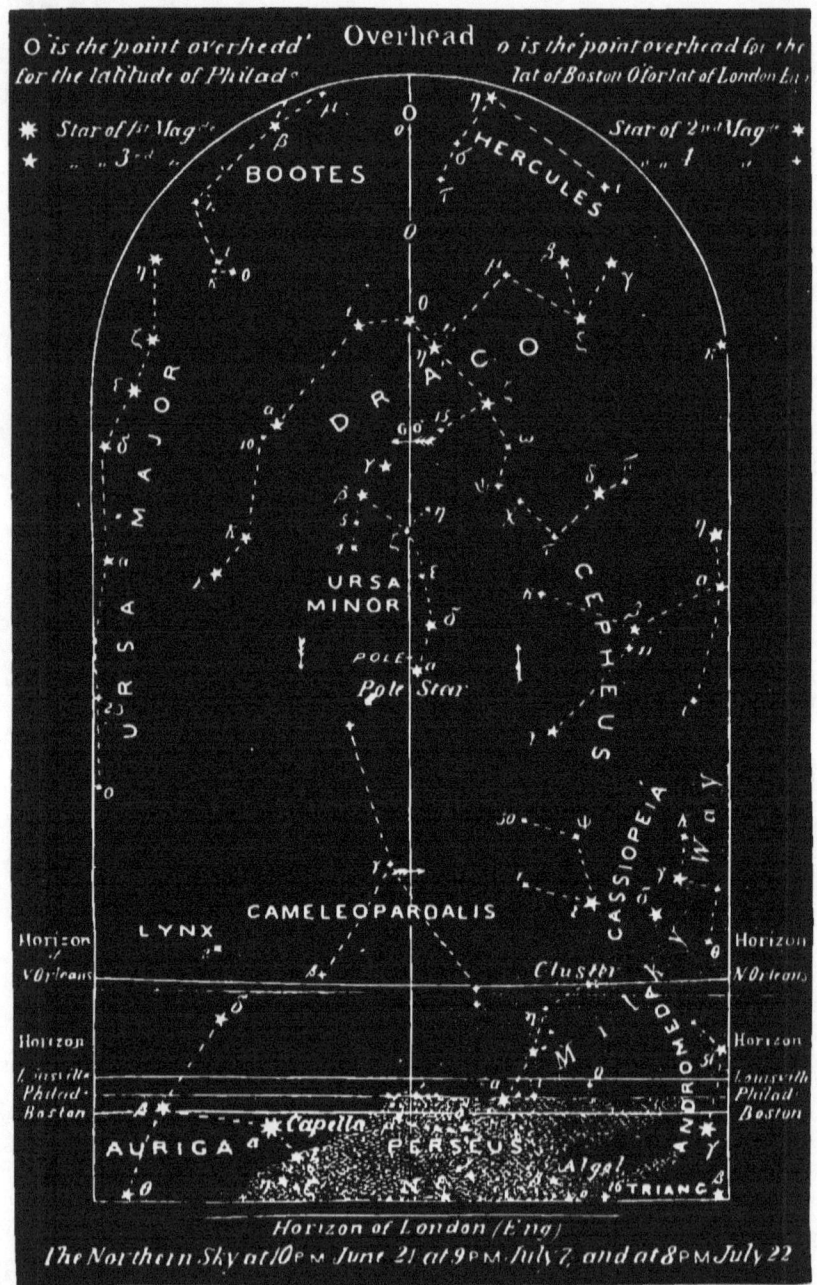

THE NORTHERN MAP FOR JULY.

149

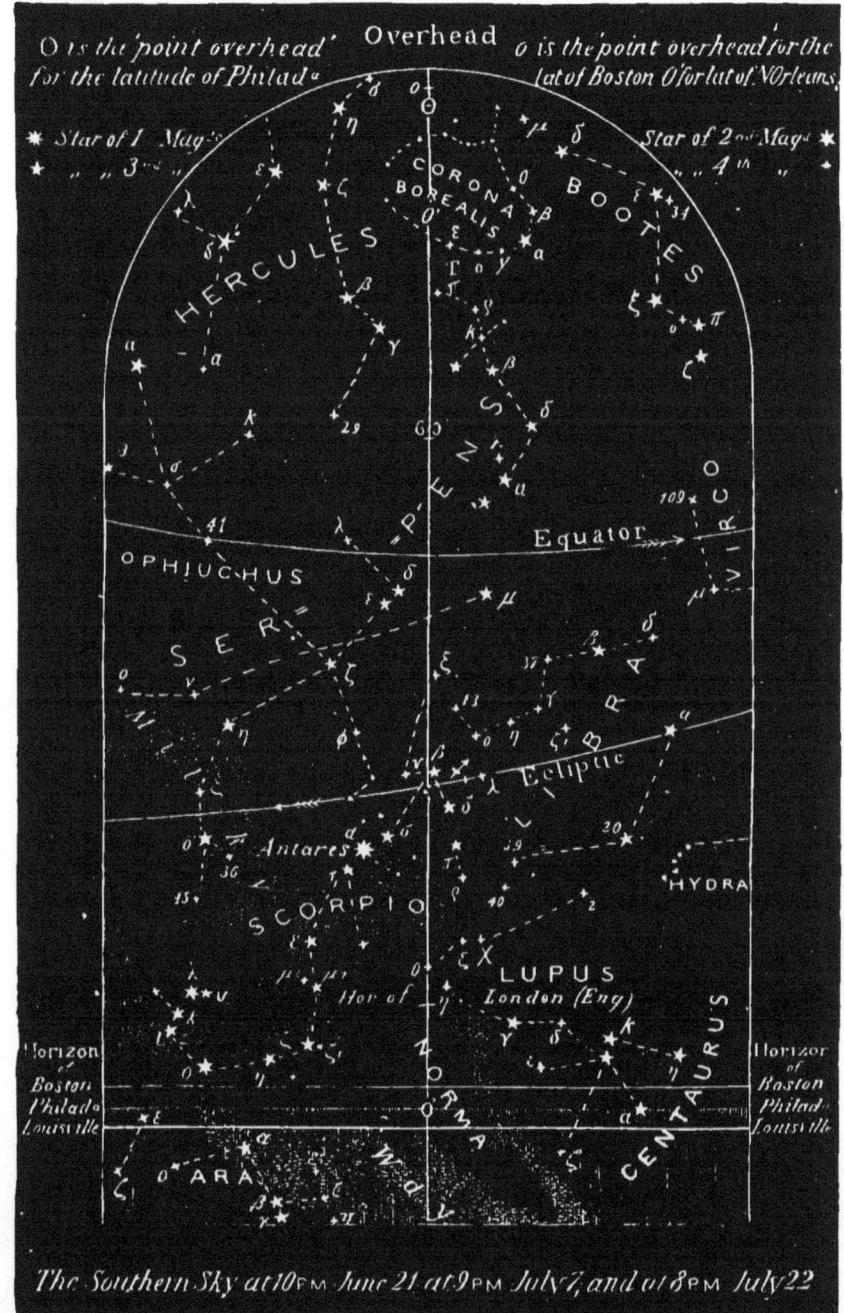

**THE SOUTHERN MAP FOR JULY.**

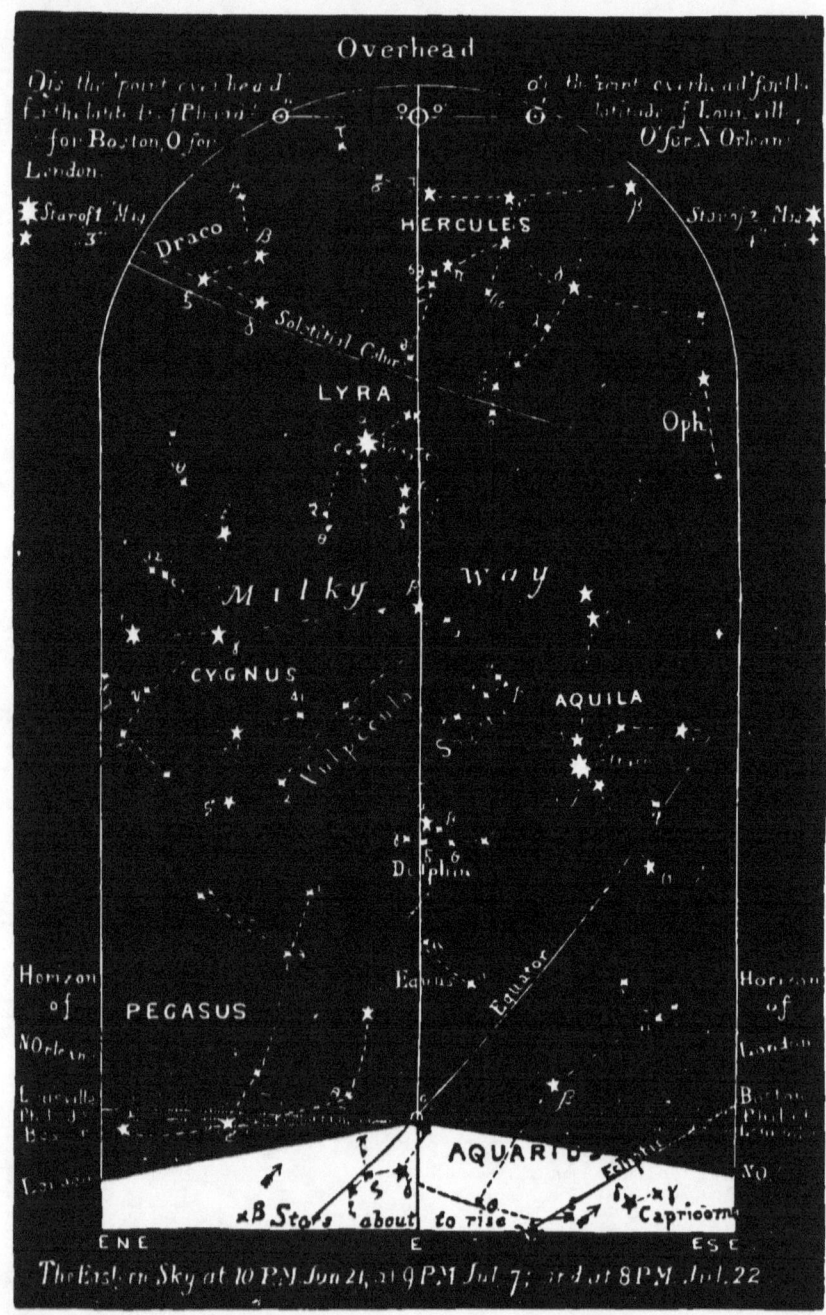

**THE EASTERN MAP FOR JULY.**

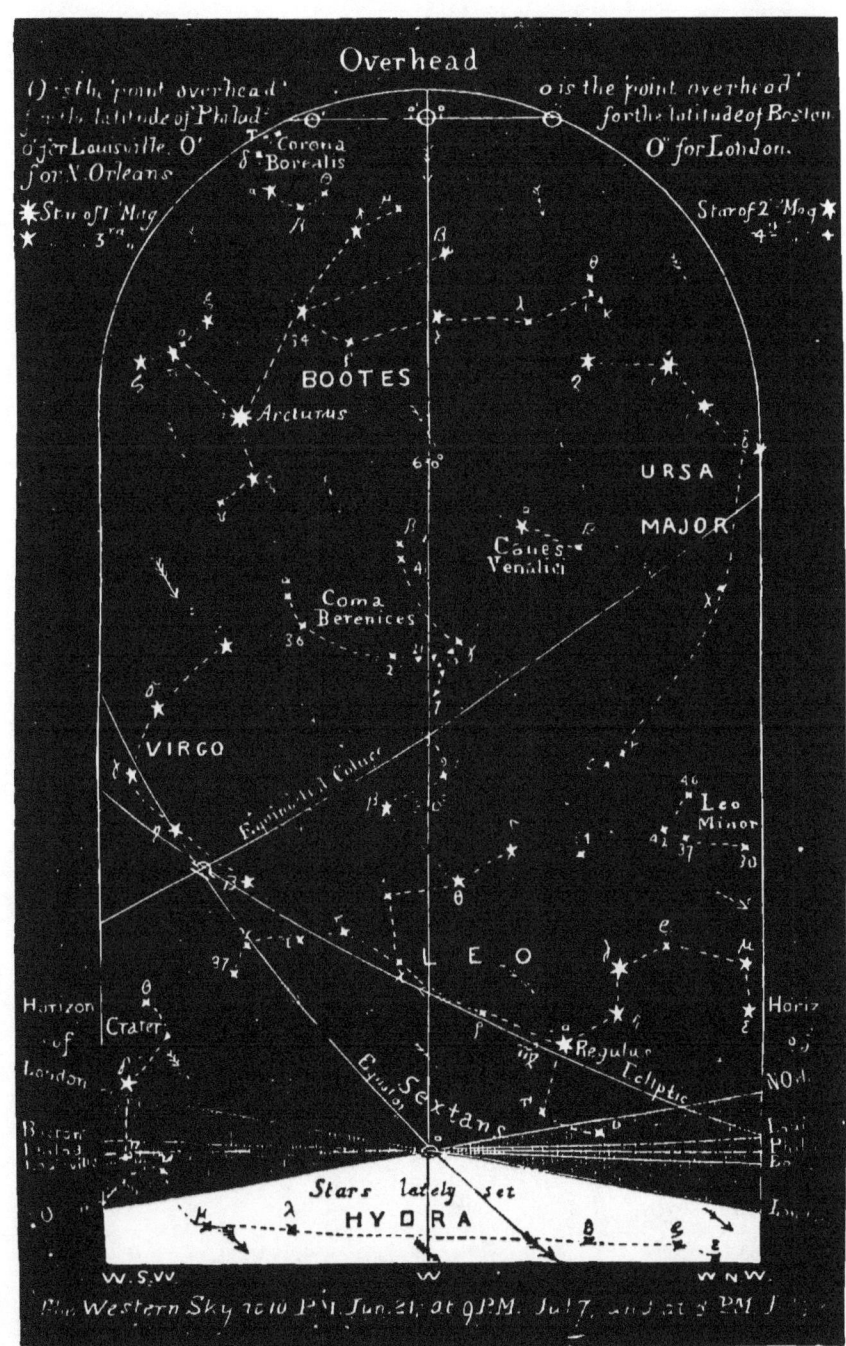

THE WESTERN MAP FOR JULY.

# THE STARS FOR AUGUST.

The northern sky (p. 164) below the pole is now chiefly remarkable for the absence of large stars. It has always seemed to me that this large, desolate region of the sky is full of meaning, and that when the architecture of the heavens comes to be rightly understood, we shall find why it is that this region is thus barren. That the feature is not accidental I am satisfied from a number of experiments I have made on the scattering of points.

The head of the Dragon is now almost exactly above the pole. Not far from the point overhead shines the beautiful steel-blue star Vega.

Although the map shows a part of Auriga (the Charioteer), and notably the bright star Capella, yet only the star $\delta$ of this constellation can be seen in America at the hours named below the map; nor can even this star be seen from places south of the latitude of Nashville (Tenn.), or thereabouts.

The ruling constellation of the zodiac this month (p. 165) is Sagittarius (the Archer). In Fig. 23 (p. 142), his bow-arm, bow, and arrow appear. I do not think it is necessary to give a full picture of this worthy. He is commonly presented as a centaur, though it is not easy to imagine the figure of a centaur among the stars of this constellation. The bow, however, is fairly well marked.

Admiral Smyth tells us that, in the days of Eratosthenes, the constellation Sagittarius was pictured as a satyr; and so it appears on the Farnese globe.

From places in the latitude of New Orleans, the constellation Ara, or "the Altar," can be partly seen. In England, as may be seen by the position of the horizon of London, we not only see no part of this constellation, but a large part of the curved tail of Scorpio is hidden from our view.

The constellation Ara, though now so far south that it cannot be seen from the latitude of Philadelphia, nor *entirely* from any latitude north of 29° S., belongs to the 48 of Ptolemy's time, and was formerly well raised above the horizon of places in latitude 40° S. That reeling of the earth, like a top, of which I have already spoken—a movement having for its period nearly 25,900 years—has, within the last 4,000 years or so (the probable age of the old constellations), so shifted the position of the earth's axis in space,* that this constellation has been thrown out of view from places whence, at the beginning of these 4,000 years, it could be well seen. Probably it was some later astronomer, who had never seen this constellation, who first

---

* The young reader must not here fall into the mistake of supposing that the position of the axis in the earth itself has changed in this way. This mistake is commonly made, and not by young learners, who may well be excused for falling into it, but by persons who suppose themselves in a position to teach. For instance: In Jules Verne's entertaining story, "Captain Hatteras," the following passage occurs, in which this error is introduced: "'I told you,' resumed the doctor, who took as much pleasure in giving as the others did in receiving instruction —'I told you that the pole was motionless in comparison with the rest of the globe. Well, that is not quite true!' 'What!' said Bell, 'has that got to be taken back?' 'Yes, Bell, the pole is not always exactly in the same place; formerly the North Star was farther from the celestial pole than it is now. So our pole has a certain motion; it describes a circle in about 26,000 years. This comes from the precession of the equinoxes, of which I shall speak soon.'" The actual effect of the precession of the equinoxes may be thus illustrated. Imagine a top shaped like a ball, spinning rapidly on its axis, and very slowly reeling,

made the mistake of drawing it upside down. As this constellation was never seen except when due south, just above the horizon, it is certain that it must have been imagined, by those who formed it, as standing an upright altar in the south. But modern pictures draw it so that, at the only time when it was visible, it would have had to be imagined as having its top with the flaming wood upon it just touching the horizon, while its base would have been above. This is so absurd that I ventured, some eleven years ago, in a set of drawings of the constellation figures, to set the altar on its base again. I was confirmed in my opinion that this was right, by the fact that on the Farnese globe, and in a chart of Geruvigus (Harleian MS., 64) the altar is represented in this upright position. Besides, the old astronomical poet, Aratus describes the Centaur as laying *on* the altar (not absurdly applying to its inverted base) the body of some beast unnamed—the modern Lupus; while Manlius, a Latin poet (who wrote probably in the reign of Tiberius), speaks of the altar as "*bearing* fire of frankincense, pictured by stars" (*Ara ferens thuris stellis imitantibus ignem*). An inverted altar cannot "bear" anything. Besides, you can see how the smoke of the fire really is pictured by the Milky Way, when once the top of the altar is set toward $a$, or upward.

its axis being inclined about $23\frac{1}{2}$ degrees from the vertical, or toward a point rather more than one-fourth of the way from the point overhead toward the horizon. Let this spinning and reeling ball be carried round a much larger globe, glowing with light and heat, to represent the sun. Then, if the ball turns $365\frac{1}{4}$ times on its axis while it is going once round the large globe, and reels so slowly that it could be carried 25,868 times round the large globe in making a single complete reel, it would illustrate the earth's motion of rotation (or spinning) once a day, of revolution (or of being carried round the sun) once a year, and of precession (or reeling) once in 25,868 years. The poles of the earth no more change than the position of the axis of a top within the wood; but the pole of the heavens (that is, the point toward which the axis is directed) makes a circuit once in 25,868 years, just as the point of the sky toward which the axis of a top is directed circuits once round the point overhead in each reel of the top.

Overhead are the Lyre and Hercules; but neither is well placed for observation.

We have now reached the most southerly part of the ecliptic, marked by the symbol ♑, which indicates the point where the sun, moving in the direction shown by the arrow, enters the sign Capricornus, which he does on or about December 20.

The Milky Way toward the south at this season is well worth studying. It is strange when we look at those complex branches, loops, and curdling masses, to find most of our books of astronomy still asserting that the Milky Way, is a faint stream of misty light circling the celestial sphere, and divided into two along half its length. Remembering, too, that the Milky Way is entirely made up of clustering stars, as sands on the sea-shore for multitude, each star being a sun glowing with its own inherent light and heat, startling thoughts are suggested respecting the immensity of the universe when we find *clouds* of these stars strewn through space.

Not far from the star $\xi$ of Ophiuchus is shown the place where, in 1604, a new star appeared, which shone for a while more brightly than any of the fixed stars. "It was exactly," says the account, "like one of the stars except that, in the vividness of its lustre and the quickness of its sparkling, it exceeded anything Kepler had ever seen before. It was every moment changing into some of the colours of the rainbow, as yellow, orange, purple, and red, though it was generally white when it was at some distance from the vapours of the horizon." These changes of colour were, of course, due entirely to our own air. Similar changes can always be seen in the colour of a star shining near the horizon, as you can see by observing Antares. Kepler's star only preserved its full lustre for about three weeks, after which it gradually grew fainter, until towards the end of 1605 it disappeared.

Pegasus (the Winged Horse), the constellation which has risen above the eastern horizon (p. 168) at the hours mentioned under the maps for this month, is the same which, eight months ago, was above the western horizon. (The actual point of the star-sphere rising at any moment in the east—that is, due east—is of course the same which six months before had been, or six months after will be, passing below the western horizon at the same hour of the day; but as a star-group of considerable size may be an hour or two in clearing the horizon, either rising or setting, it may be seven or eight months before a constellation which had been just wholly above the western horizon is seen wholly above the eastern horizon at the same hour.) It will be observed—and the point is well worth careful noting—that the position

Fig. 24.—Boötes and Corona Borealis.

of Pegasus is entirely changed from that which it had occupied before it began to pass below the western horizon in January. Then the head of Pegasus was close to the horizon, and on the left as you stood facing the west. Now, though his head lies towards the left, it is much higher above the horizon than the winged back. In both cases, however, the horse is represented in an unnatural position, or at least in a position which a horse could only assume by accident. But then a winged horse may, perhaps, be considered free to assume any attitude he pleases, to have his head or his back lowest at will—his feet on this side or that or flourishing upwards. Again, observe that now in the east, Aquarius (the Water Bearer), as yet, however, only partially above the horizon, lies to the right of Pegasus; whereas in January Aquarius had already completely set at the same hours. On the other hand, Cetus has not yet risen in the east even in part (the Sea Monster will begin to show a part of his vast bulk next month); whereas in January the whole of this constellation was above the horizon, but towards the south-west, so as not to fall into the western map for that month.

The Milky Way, where it crosses the eastern sky, is full of beauty and interest. It is singularly bright in the space between the stars $\beta$, $\gamma$, and $\delta$ of the constellation Cygnus.

In the west (p. 169) there is little specially to notice, except the noble figure presented by Boötes (the Herdsman) (Fig. 24), now more favourably placed for study as a constellation than at any other season of the year.

# STAR MAPS FOR AUGUST.

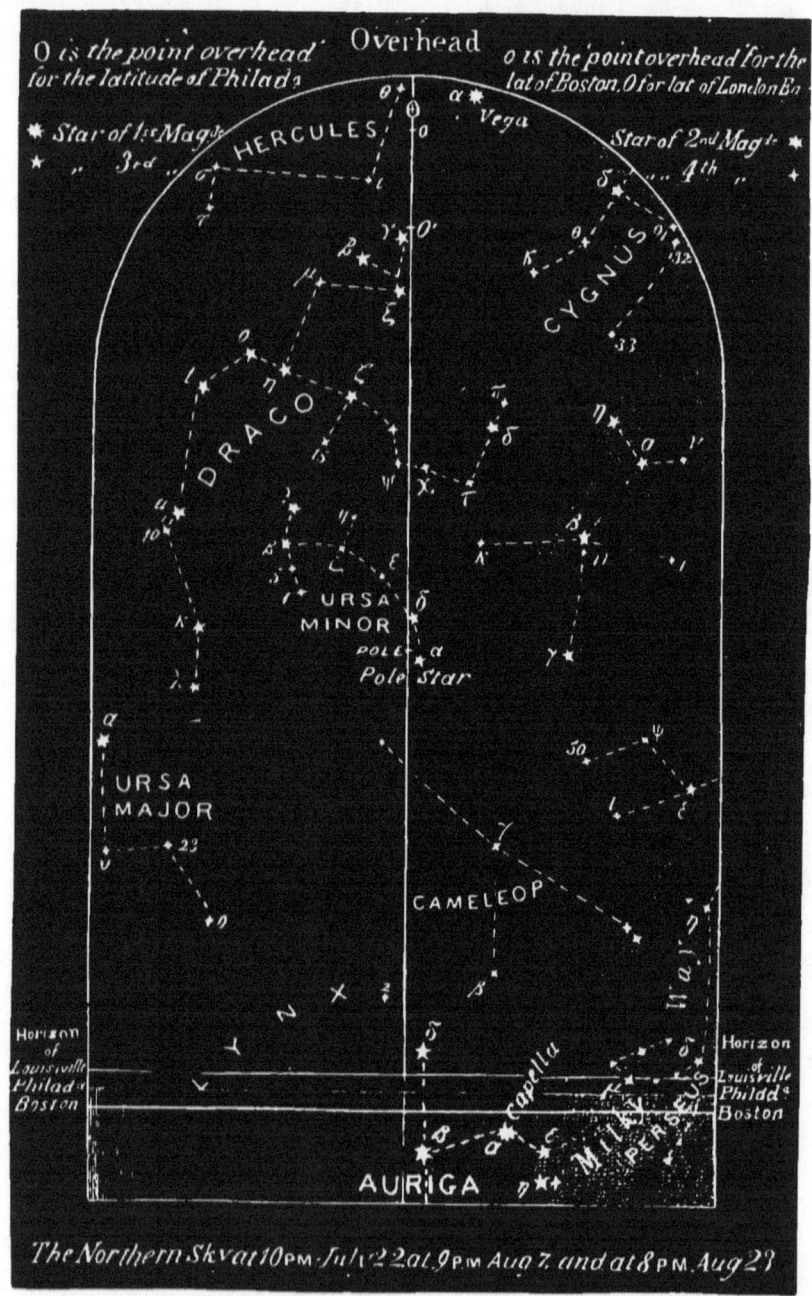

THE NORTHERN MAP FOR AUGUST.

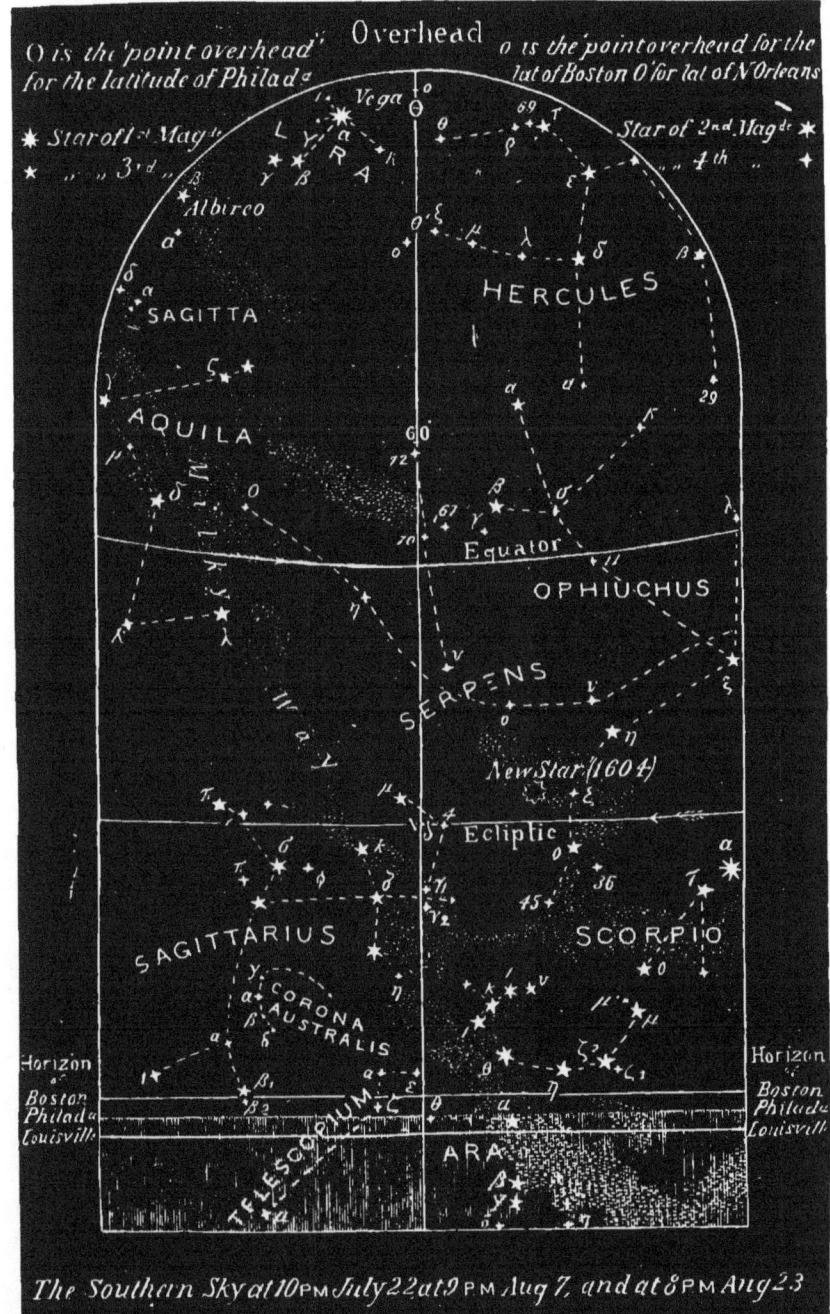

THE SOUTHERN MAP FOR AUGUST.

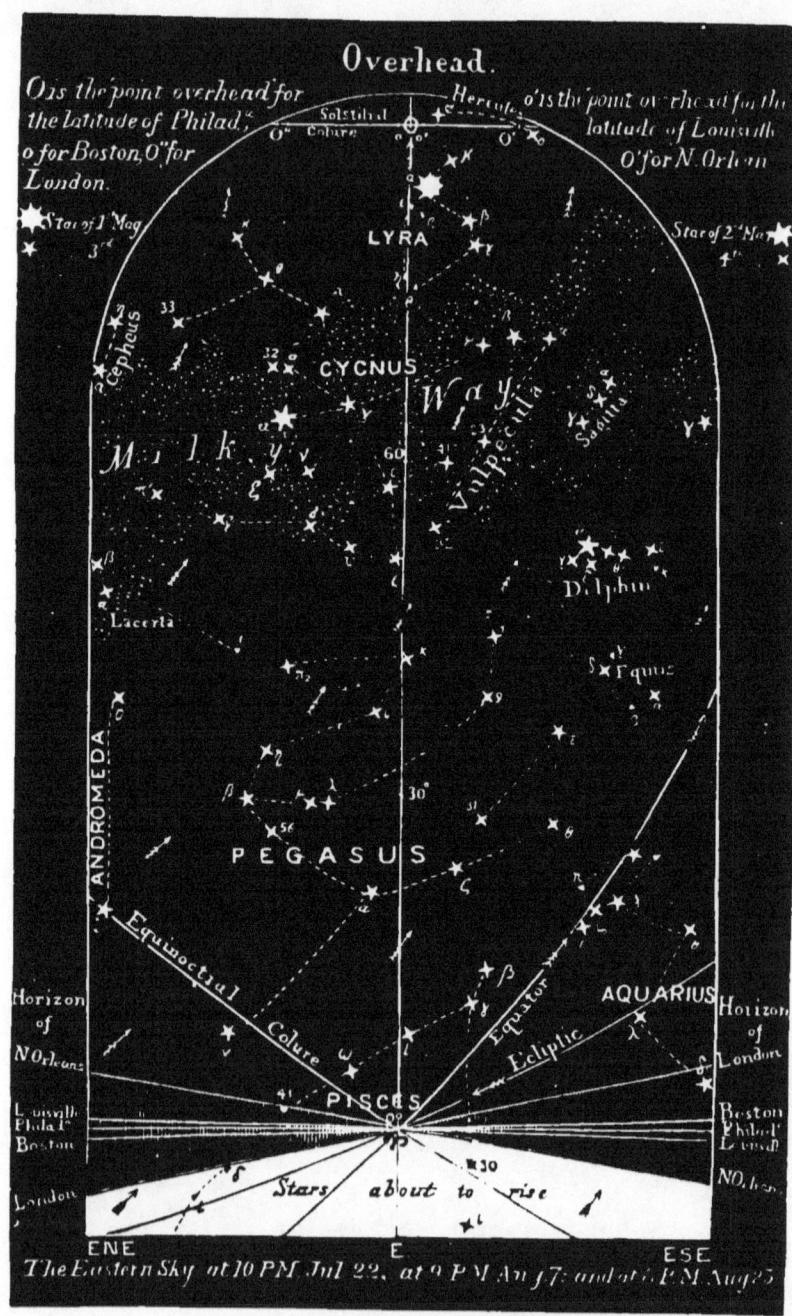

**THE EASTERN MAP FOR AUGUST.**

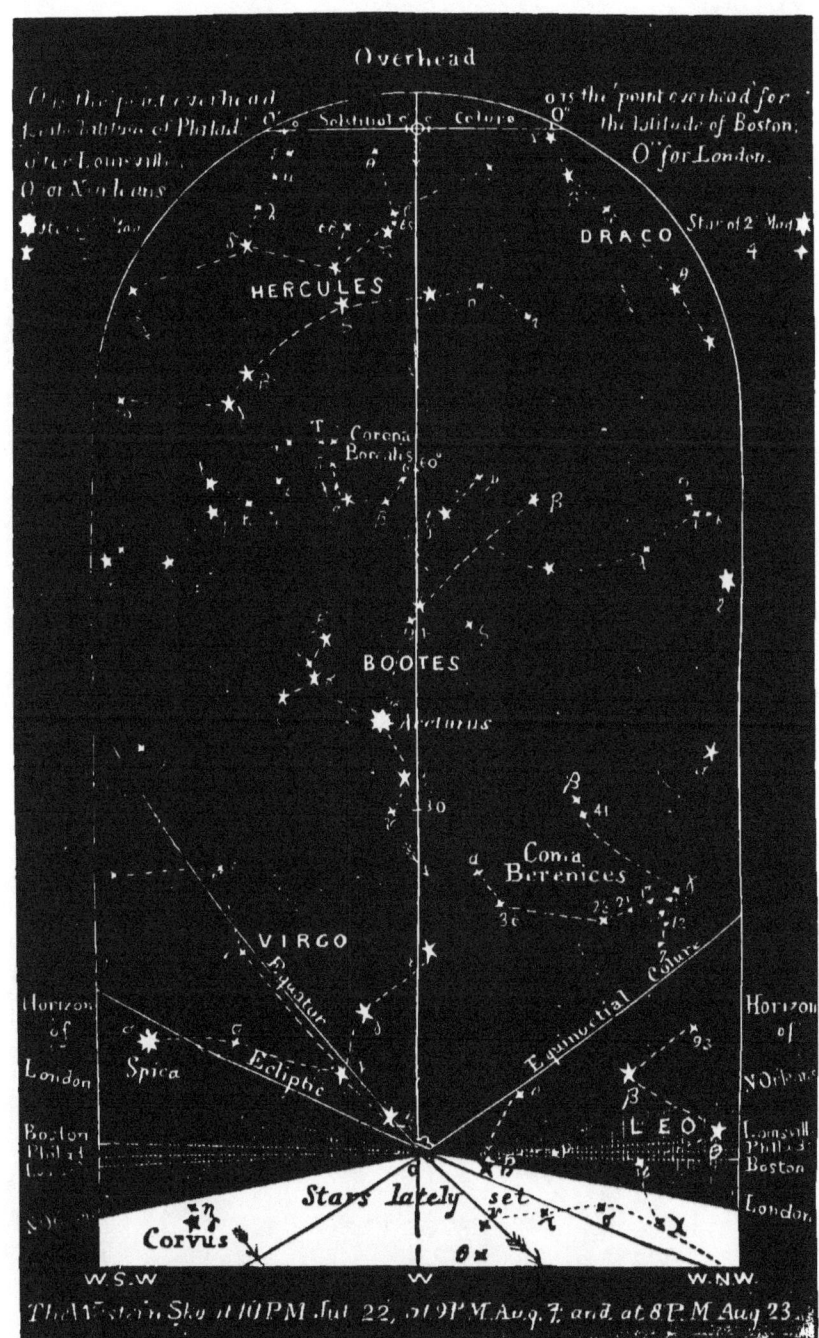

THE WESTERN M P FOR AUGUST.

# THE STARS FOR SEPTEMBER.

THE Great Bear (p. 182) is now approaching the north again, low down. The two forward stars of the Plough, or Dipper, *a* and *β*, can be seen in our northern map for the hours named, low down on the left; but I remind the learner that,

Fig. 25.—Aquarius, Capricornus, and Piscis Australis.

so far as the Plough is concerned, the picture illustrating the opening pages about "A Clock in the Sky," is the one to be studied. The Little Bear is now descending on the left or west side of the pole.

In the southern heavens (p. 183) we find two ecliptical constellations dividing the honours of the night, Sagittarius (the Archer) and Capricornus (the Sea Goat), Fig. 25. Sagittarius needs no special mention this month after what I said of him in the last section.

Capricornus was formerly the constellation entered by the sun on the shortest day of the year, when he is farthest south of the equator, and about to begin his return toward it. You will see that at present the constellation includes the ascending sign, marked ♒ for Aquarius (the Water-Bearer) (The symbol is placed on the right or west of the division of the ecliptic to which it belongs.) A strange superstition was entertained by the old astrologers, that whenever all the planets come together in Capricornus there is a deluge. Some said, indeed, that the Flood had been occasioned by such a conjunction, and that when all the planets come together in Cancer the world will be destroyed by fire. I suppose the origin of the superstition was somewhat on this wise : They saw that when the sun, one of the planets of the astrological system, was in Cancer his rays were warmest ; when he was in Capricorn, his rays were feeblest, and the air usually damp and cold. If such effects followed when one planet was in these constellations, much more might heat be expected when several of the planets were together in Cancer, and floods of rain when several were together in Capricorn. But when *all* were together in either constellation, then the greatest heat or the worst floods possible might be expected. The tradition is a very ancient one indeed. Admiral Smyth attributes its invention to the astrologers of the Middle Ages; but in reality it was due to the Chaldean astronomers, and is found in company with a statement that they had observed the heavens for 470,000 years, during which time they had calculated the nativity of all the children who had been born. It is not absolutely necessary, however, that you should believe this. For my own part, I think it quite possible that they omitted some of the children born during that long period.

Capricornus is usually represented as a fish-tailed goat, the head and horns where the two stars α and β are marked, the feet (fore-feet) at ψ, the tail flourishing off toward γ and δ.

Higher up in the heavens we see the fine constellation Aquila or "the Eagle," usually represented in modern maps as shown in Fig. 26. Formerly a figure of the Bithynian youth, Antinous, was included in this constellation; but he is now generally omitted. Parts of the Milky Way, near and in this constellation, are very bright, and even with a small telescope seem to be crowded with stars.

Close to Aquila is the pretty little constellation the Dolphin, called Delphinus, or, perhaps better,—as in my

Fig 26.—Aquila.

ilas,—Delphin, which is as good Latin and shorter. This little group really shows some degree of resemblance to the animal whose name has been given to it, though our modern maps do not picture a real dolphin, but a creature, as Admiral Smyth well remarks, resembling rather a huge periwinkle pulled out of its shell; and certainly not "very like a whale." He quotes a curious blunder of certain Orientalists, who, finding the old Hindu name of the group to signify a sea-hog, considered it was not meant to be a fish at all; but the Hindu "sea-hog" was the porpoise. Indeed, the French name, from which our word porpoise is derived, shows that the resemblance has struck others besides the

Hindus—that name being *porc-poisson*, or hog-fish. Smyth himself has made an amusing mistake about the two stars Alpha and Beta of the Dolphin, which bear the pleasing names, Svalocin and Rotanev. Of the first epithet, which he call "cacophonous and barbaric," he remarks that "no poring into the black-letter versions of the Almagest, El Battàni, Ibn Yúnis, and other authorities, enables one to form any rational conjecture as to the misreading, miswriting, or misapplication, in which so strange a metamorphosis could have originated." Of *Rotanev* he simply says that this barbarous term "putteth derivation and etymology at defiance." If he could but have found Arabic meanings for these words, as delightful a story might have resulted as that about Mr. Pickwick's great prize, the stone bearing the inscription—

    **BILST**
   **UMPSHI**
   **SMARK**

or the true story of "Keip on this Syde," mentioned in the "Antiquary" in connection with the stone inscribed A. K. L. L. for Aiken Drum's Lang Ladle. The real explanation of the name Svalocin and Rotanev is very simple. The names first appear in the Palermo Catalogue. The name of the chief assistant there was Nicolo Cacciatore, or Nicholas the Hunter, the Latin for which is Nicolaus Venator. Reverse these names and you get Svalocin and Rotanev. Mr. Webb (whose "Celestial Objects for Common Telescopes" every student should possess) seems to have been the first to explain Signor Cacciatore's little puzzle. He truly says that if the above account is not the right key, it is certainly a marvel that it should open the lock so readily.

 Above Aquila we see Sagitta (the Arrow), the smallest of the ancient constellations. The present appearance of the stars forming this small group does not very startlingly impress the idea of an arrow upon one. Possibly the stars have somewhat changed in brightness and in relative position since the group was named. In fact, we know that all the stars are rushing with enormous velocity through space, and though they seem to change very slowly indeed in their position in the heavens, so that most of the constellations have changed very little even during the 4,000 years which have passed since they were mapped, yet a small group like Sagitta would show the effects of such changes readily enough after a few thousand years. It is at least two thousand, and probably four thousand, years old.

The neighbouring constellation, Vulpecula et Anser, or "the Fox and the Goose," on the other hand, is not an old one but was formed by Hevelius (small thanks to him). "I wished," he says, "to place a fox with a goose in the space of sky well fitted to it; because such an animal is very cunning, voracious, and fierce." (This is a reason, indeed.) "Aquila and Vultur" (Lyra, "the Lyre," was sometimes called Vultur Cadens, "the Swooping Vulture") "are of the same nature, rapacious and greedy." He might have reasoned equally well that Anser (the Goose,) was fitly placed near Cygnus (the Swan), and that the Arrow (Sagitta), which had passed over the Eagle's head, might be regarded as fairly aimed for the Fox. The real fact is, I suppose, that Hevelius was determined to fit in a constellation of his own in this space between Sagitta and Cygnus, and was prepared to be content with any argument, good, bad, or indifferent, in favour of his plan.

For shortness, the constellation may be conveniently called Vulpecula, or, as in my large atlas, *Vulpes*—that is, the Fox, instead of "the Little Fox."

In Vulpecula there is a remarkable object called the Dumb-bell nebula, or star-cloud. It cannot be seen without a telescope, and a powerful telescope is required to show the object as pictured in Fig. 27. It was formerly thought to consist entirely of small stars, so remote that they could not be separately discerned; but it has lately been discovered that the greater part of this nebula's light comes from glowing gas. The vastness of the space occupied by this cloud of luminous gas will be understood—though no mind can possibly conceive it—when I mention that at the distance of the nearest of the fixed stars the whole of our solar system would appear but as a mere point, even in a powerful telescope. The Dumb-bell nebula covers quite a large space as seen in such an instrument. It is also, probably, much farther away than the nearest fixed stars. It must, therefore occupy a region of space exceeding many times that through which the planets of our solar system pursue their paths. Yet the span of our earth's path around the sun is fully one hundred and eighty-four millions of miles; while Neptune—the remotest planet of the solar system—travels thirty times farther from the sun, having thus an orbit spanning more than five thousand millions of miles. A globe just fitting the path of Neptune would contain many quadrillions of cubic miles,—and probably the Dumb-bell nebula exceeds such a globe in volume (or to speak more exactly, occupies a space exceeding such a globe in volume) many millions of times.

Fig. 27.—The Dumb-Bell Nebula.

Very strange is the thought that astronomers should have been able to find out what this mighty mass of glowing gas consists of. Placed yonder amid the glories of the Milky Way, lost to human vision through its vast remoteness, only brought within our view at all by means of powerful telescopes, and only revealing its true shape when seen with the most powerful telescopes men have yet constructed, what at first sight can seem more amazing than that men should be able to tell what kind of substance it is which gives out the misty lustre of that cloudlet in space? The very light which comes to us from the Dumb-bell nebula has probably taken hundreds of years in crossing the tremendous space separating us from that object. Yet that light has conveyed its message truly. Examined with that instrument, the spectroscope, the light of the Dumb-bell nebula presents, not the rainbow-tinted streak which comes from glowing solid and liquid bodies, but three bright lights only. At least three lines are seen if the nebula is examined through a fine slit; if the field of view is opened, there are seen three faint images of the cloudlet. The correct way of describing what the spectroscope tells us about this object is to say that, instead of its light presenting all the colours of the rainbow, it is found, when sifted by the spectroscope, to contain three colours only, all of them greenish, but slightly different in tint. One of the colours is precisely such a tint of green as comes (with four other colours) from glowing hydrogen gas, and shows us that there are enormous masses of hydrogen in that remote cloud; another tint shows, in like manner, that there are immense masses of nitrogen; but the third tint has not yet been found to correspond with a tint emitted by any known substance. The skein of light from that double fluff-ball has thus been unravelled by the spectroscope, after journeying millions of millions of miles and has been sorted into three tints, two of which have been matched against the known tints of earthly gases, but the third remains as yet unmatched.

In the east (p. 186) the square of Pegasus is the most conspicuous feature. Its position should be carefully compared with that which it occupied in January in the western sky. The line joining the two Alphas, now nearly horizontal, was then nearly vertical. Andromeda now occupies the position above Aries referred to in Milton's well-known lines :

> " Such wonder seized, though after Heav'n seen,
> The Spirit malign, but much more envy seized,
> At sight of all this world beheld so fair,
> Round he surveys (and well might, where he stood,
> So high above the circling canopy
> Of night's extended shade), from eastern point
> Of Libra to the fleecy star that bears
> Andromeda far off Atlantic seas
> Beyond the horizon."

In the western skies (p. 187) the fine position of Boötes is worth noticing. The figure is now nearly upright, and though our latitude is much farther north than that of the astronomers who first devised the constellations, yet (owing partly to the change in the position of the pole of the heavens, correcting the effect of difference of latitude) we now see Boötes the Herdsman chasing the Great Bear towards the north, much as in all probability he was imagined by those who invented these fine constellations. To make his figure complete, however, as Boötes the Shouter, we ought to include the stars of the northern crown as forming part of his figure. So imagined, this constellation seems to me second only to Orion in suggestiveness.

# STAR MAPS FOR SEPTEMBER

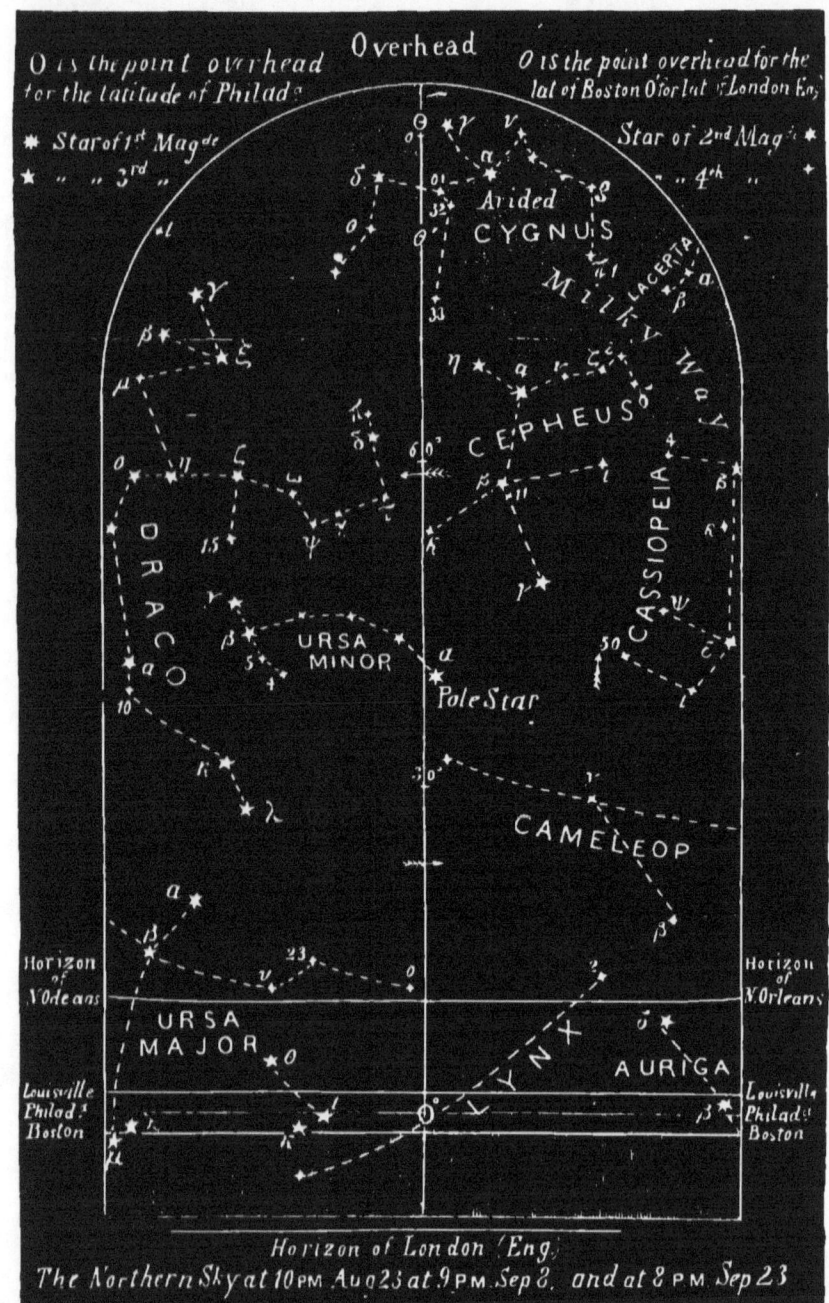

THE NORTHERN MAP FOR SEPTEMBER.

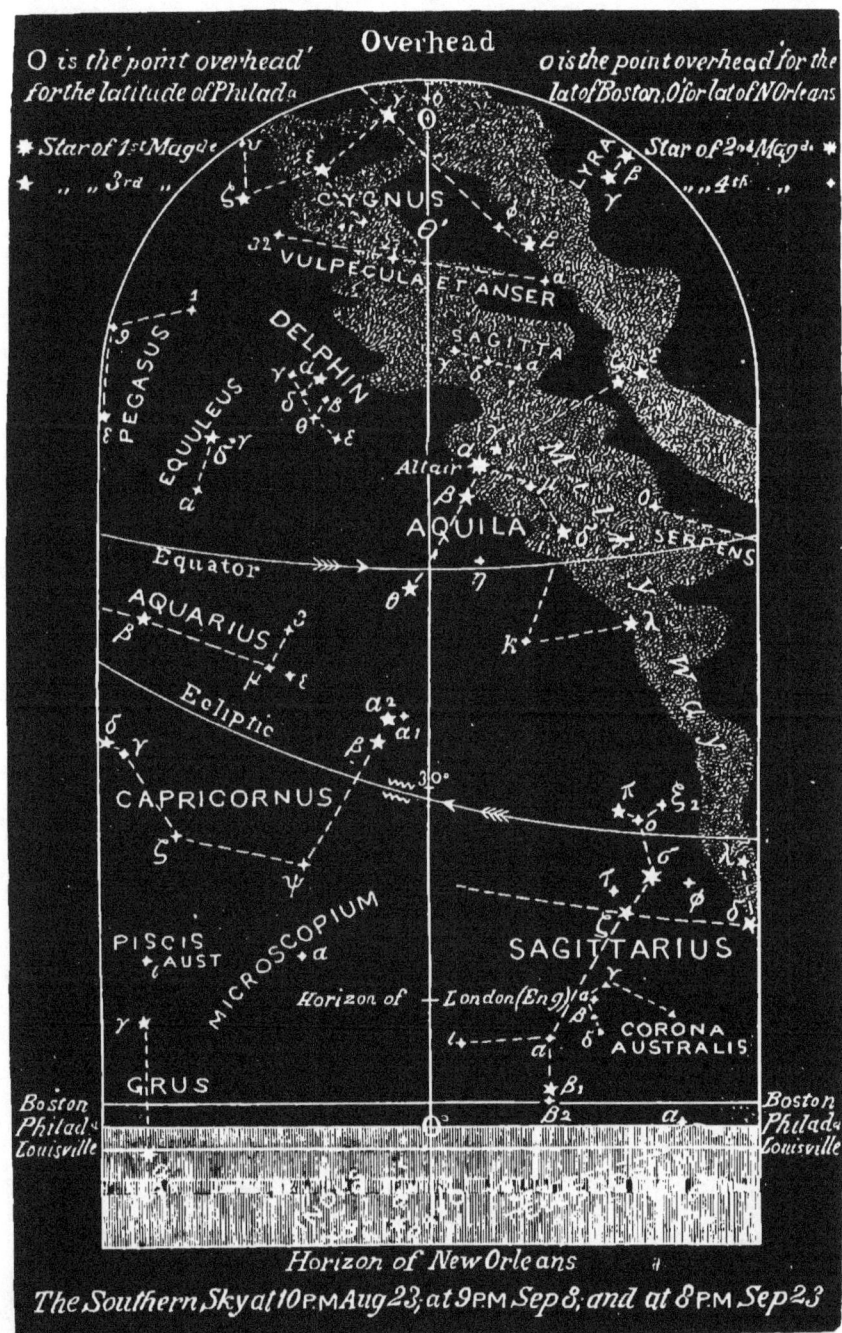

THE SOUTHERN MAP FOR SEPTEMBER.

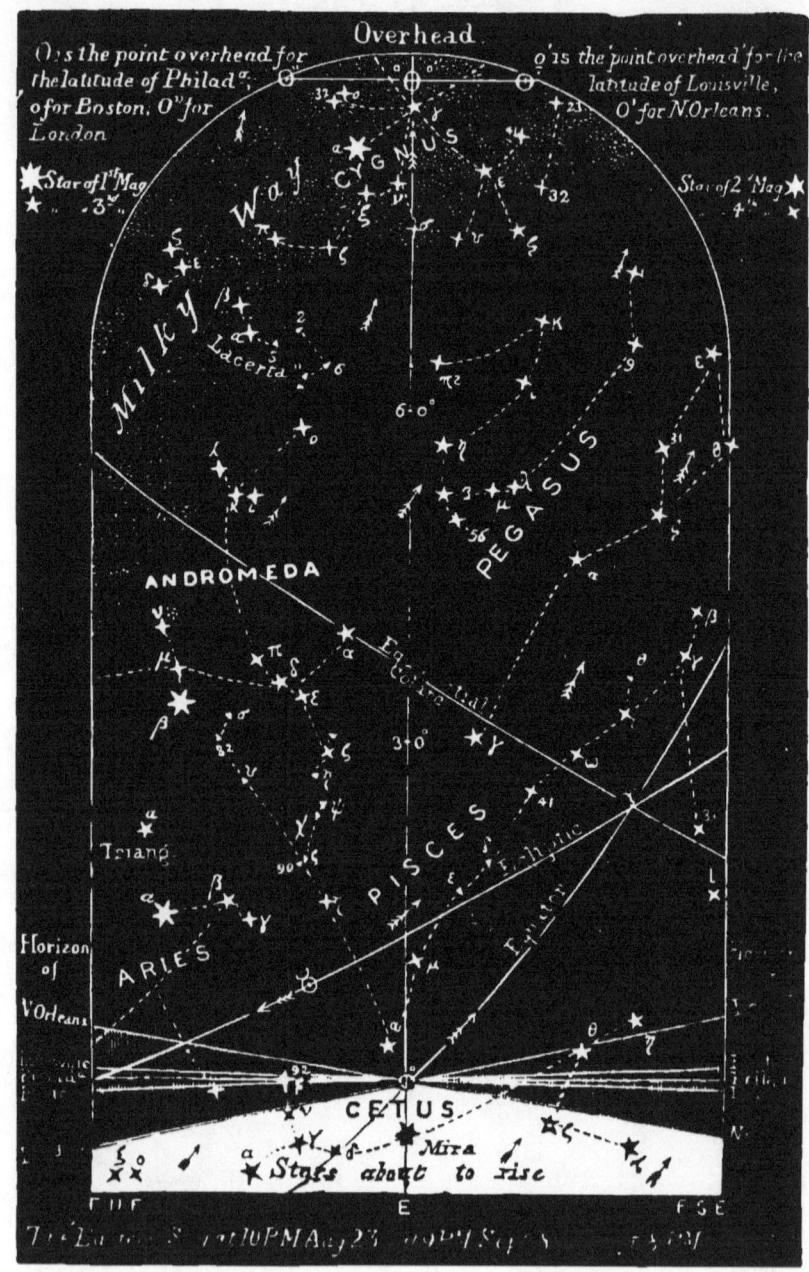

THE EASTERN MAP FOR SEPTEMBER.

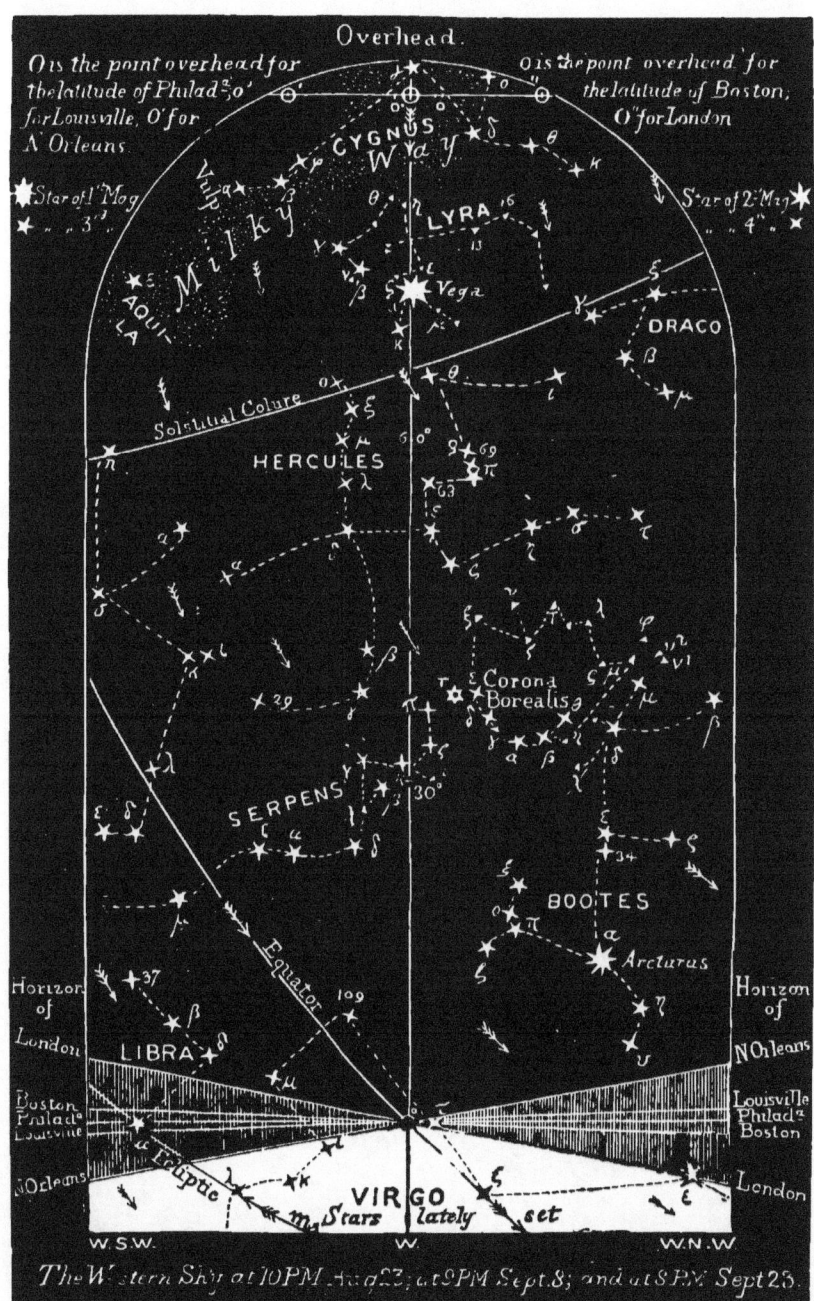

**THE WESTERN MAP FOR SEPTEMBER.**

# THE STARS FOR OCTOBER.

### The Plough, or Dipper.

I propose now to give a brief account of the seven bright stars of the Plough, or Dipper, as they really are, not merely as they appear in the sky. I take them as the most convenient, and in several respects also as the best, illustration of what applies in reality (with changes in matters of detail) to all the thousands of stars we see, and to thousands of times as many stars which only the telescope reveals to us.

When you look during the evenings of this month at the stars of this group, seen low down toward the north, in the position shown in Map I. for the month, you see seven small points of brilliant light,—each of them seems like the "little star" in the familiar nursery rhyme. If the eye were a perfect optical instrument, and the air were perfectly transparent and still, and if, also, light instead of travelling to us in waves of many lengths, gave us an exactly truthful account of what is out yonder in space, even the seven little stars we see would be very much reduced in seeming size. They would appear as mere points. The most powerful telescope men have yet made, and probably the most powerful telescope men ever will make, would not show these seven stars larger than points, such that the human eye could perceive no breadth in those minute disks. Such are the stars, even the leading ones, to the natural eye. In the mind's eye, however, these seven stars are very different objects. I am not going to draw on my imagination in what I am about to tell you. I am not going to show what these stars *may* be, but to describe what science assures us that they *are*.

### Sizes of the Stars of the Plough, or Dipper.

In the first place, then, every one of these seven points of light is an enormous globe, not only larger than the earth on which we live, but thousands or rather hundreds of thousands of times larger. How large they really are we do not know; we do not even know how far away they are; but we *do* know they are so far away that our sun removed and set beside the nearest of them would not look so bright as the faintest of the seven. They *may* be so far away that our sun removed to their distance would scarce be seen at all, or would even require a powerful telescope to show him; but that he would not be so bright as Delta, the middle one, and the faintest of the seven, is certain. In considering what this means, you should remember that the sun himself looks only a small body. We might well believe, so far as appearances are concerned, that he is no larger than the moon, and the moon no larger than yonder hill that hides her from our view as she sets. But the sun is in reality a globe exceeding our earth one million and a quarter times in volume. If such a globe as our earth, only, were set aglow with a brightness so great that every part of her surface shone more resplendently than the piece of lime used in the calcium lantern (and one cannot easily *look* at that piece of lime so glowing), and this enormous mass of white-hot fire were set travelling away toward the nearest star of the Plough, it would be utterly lost to view before it had traversed a fiftieth part of the distance!

### Their Composition.

Secondly, every one of the seven stars consists of matter like that in our sun, glowing with intense lustre. When we use the instrument called the spectroscope, distance does not prevent us from recognizing vapours of various kinds in the atmosphere of a luminous body so long as the light reaches us in sufficient amount. In the case of the stars, distant though they are, we get the same sort of information. And thus we learn that iron, sodium, magnesium, calcium, hydrogen, and others of our familiar elements exist in the atmospheres of the stars, just as we have found that they exist in the atmosphere of our own sun. These seven stars, like our sun and their fellow-suns, are great masses of intensely hot matter, all around which there lies a deep atmosphere of glowing gases, including in the vapourous form many of those elements, such as our metals, which the greatest heat we can use serves only to melt, not to turn into vapour.* You know that at a certain low degree of heat water is solid, at ordinary heat it becomes fluid, and at a great heat—much hotter than the greatest the hand can bear—water turns into steam or vapour. Iron only becomes fluid at a heat far greater than that at which water boils. You can imagine, then, how intense the heat must be at which molten iron turns into iron-steam. But in the sun and in his fellow-suns the stars, iron, and substances still more stubborn in their resistance to heat, are turned into the form of vapour. The *air* of every star is a mixture of iron-steam, zinc-steam, calcium-steam, and many other such fiery vapours, besides hydrogen; and all these vapours are so hot that they shine with their own inherent lustre. Imagine an atmosphere such as this, where the clouds which form are metallic drops, and the rains which fall are sheets of molten metals!

* I must mention—without explaining, however—that by means of electricity, the most stubborn metals can be vapourized in small quantities, and for a brief space of time. But I am speaking above of such heat as we obtain in furnaces.

## Their Motion.

But thirdly,—and this is the point to which I want chiefly to direct your attention,—every one of these seven suns is in swift motion. It was formerly supposed that the fixed stars really were at rest, because year after year, and century after century, passed without showing any change in their position. But gradually—even before the telescope was much used in observing the places of stars—it began to be suspected that they are slowly shifting in position on the vault of heaven. Later, very close attention was paid to the point, the telescope being used to determine the exact positions of a great number of stars, and now about 2,000 have had their slow motions on the star-vaults measured, and set down in tables for the use of astronomers employed in observatories. It occurred to me, seven or eight years

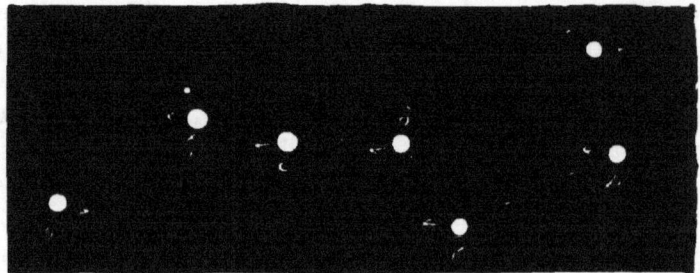

Fig. 28.—Seven stars of the Plough.

ago, that it would be interesting to picture these star-motions in maps; for tables, after all, though very pleasant in their way, are not very clear in their teachings. I made, therefore, two charts, one of all the northern stars, the other of all the southern stars, whose motions have been ascertained. These charts are given in a book of mine called "The Universe;" but a sufficient idea of the method I employed may be derived from Fig. 28, above, showing the movements of the seven stars of the Plough. The little arrows attached to the seven stars show the courses along which these stars are moving. But the length of each arrow has a meaning, too, for it is made proportional to the rate at which the star is changing its place. I have said above that the stars are in *swift* motion; and I have also spoken of the stars as *slowly* shifting in position. I think you will presently admit that both these descriptions are correct. For, first, each arrow in the figure has a length corresponding to the distance its star travels during *thirty-six thousand years.* After this enormous period, the stars will have moved from their present positions to the points of their respective arrows, so that the shape of the Plough will then be as in Fig. 29.

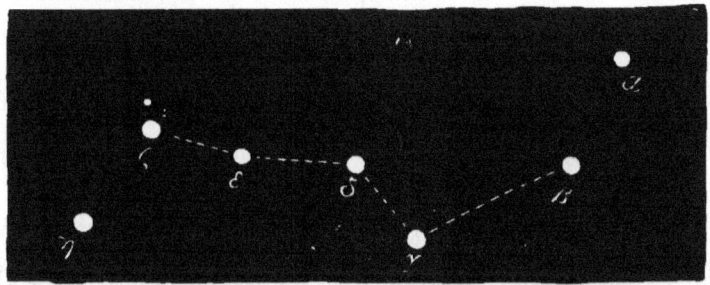

Fig. 29.—The same stars 36,000 years hence *

It will be easy for the young student now to find the shape of the Plough at any time, past or to come. Fig. 30 shows the shape it will have 100,000 years hence; Fig. 31 shows the shape it had 100,000 years ago.

Comparing Fig. 29 with Fig. 28, it cannot but be admitted that the change is small for an interval so long as 36,000

* It may be well for me, perhaps, to explain that my charts of the motions of stars in the Great Bear, etc., were published *before* M. Flammarion wrote a paper called "The Past and Future of a Constellation," in which he made use of my charts, as I have myself done above. I do not in the least mind any one's borrowing from me without acknowledging the obligation,—an omission which can easily result from carelessness,— but I do not wish it to be thought that I have myself borrowed without acknowledgment, where, in reality, I am only using my own material, gathered, by the way, at the cost of some labour.

years. Consider that, according to the usual way of reckoning, less than a fifth of this interval has elapsed since the very beginning of our history, and that all the time these slow stars have been creeping over only a sixth part

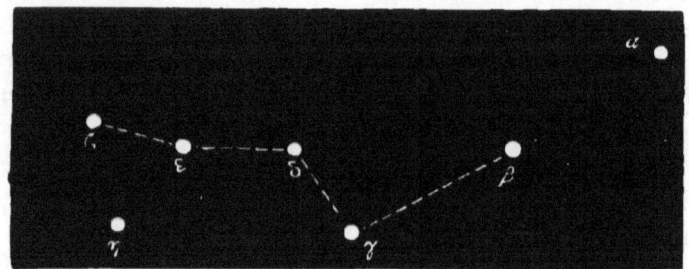

Fig. 30. The same stars 100,000 years hence.

of the short arc on the heavens which measures their motion during 36,000 years, as shown in Fig. 28.

Yet a very easy calculation will show that the same motion which is so slow when thus measured is, in reality, enormously swift. If you notice the arrows in Fig. 28, you

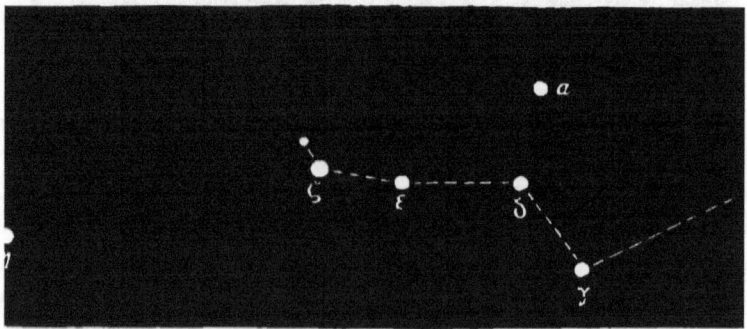

Fig. 31.—The same stars 100,000 years ago.

will see that the length of each differs very little from the distance between ζ and the companion star Jack by-the-Middle Horse. Now, this distance is equal to about half the apparent diameter of the sun. Thus, if any of these stars were at the sun's distance from us, its arrow would be equal in real length to about half the sun's diameter, or considerably more than 400,000 miles. But the nearest of all the stars is more than 200,000 times farther away than the sun; and there is every reason to believe that each one of the seven stars of the Plough is at least five times farther away than the nearest star, and probably farther away still. Thus the arrow attached to each of the seven stars represents a thwart distance of a million times 400,000 miles, or 400,000,000,000 miles at least. So that, as this distance is traversed in 36,000 years, the distance traversed each year is more than 11,000,000 miles. As there are $31\frac{1}{2}$ million seconds in a year, it follows that the thwart motion of each of these stars amounts to at least one-third of a mile per second. This is about five times the swiftness of a cannon-ball, and for a giant mass like a sun, doubtless with an attendant family of planets, represents a truly tremendous energy of motion. But probably the real distance of these seven stars is so great that their thwart motion is very much greater. We come now, however, to the most wonderful point of all.

### The Family of Five.

In all four figures, it will be noticed, the five stars, $\beta$, $\gamma$, $\delta$, $\epsilon$, $\zeta$, besides the companion star of $\zeta$, occupy much the same position. The breaking of the Plough is caused by the motions of $\alpha$ and $\eta$, not by those of the other five stars, which move as though they were all connected together and formed a single system. Noticing this, and finding that in other parts of the stellar heavens a similar phenomenon could be recognized, I was led to believe that these are really cases of drifting motions among the stars,—in other words, that there are sets or systems of stars travelling together, each as a single family, through space, and that the five stars $\beta$, $\gamma$, $\delta$, $\epsilon$, and $\zeta$, form one of these families.

Now, it so chanced that a method had recently been indicated for measuring the motions of stars from or toward us,—not the thwart motions by which they change their apparent position in the sky, but the motions by which they change their distance from us. I do not now enter into an explanation of this method, simply mentioning that the light waves as they come in from a star show by their nature whether the star is moving from or towards us, and at what rate. Here, then, was a means of testing my theory that five stars of the Plough form a single family; for if they do, then all five are, of course, receding from us, or approaching us, at the same rate. The matter was put to the test two or three years after I had suggested the trial; and it was found (by Mr. Huggins, the present President of the Astronomical Society) that the five stars are all receding at the same common rate of seventeen miles per second.

Thus, when you look at the Plough, the seven points which you see seemingly at rest, are in reality, seven splendid suns, certainly much larger, and probably very much larger, than our own; they are all raging with fiery heat and glowing with the most intense lustre; they are all rushing with inconceivable swiftness through the depths of space; and lastly, five of them, though separated from each other by millions of millions of miles, form, nevertheless, a single family (of which the companion of $\zeta$ is a subordinate member), and rush as one system through space, each attended by its own family of dependent worlds!

## The Stars for October.

And now let us turn to the stars for the month. You will note that the northern map (p. 204) requires no explanation this month, all the constellations shown in it having already been described. The map is necessary, like the northern map for the next two months, to complete the series. For the observer should be able, from his set of monthly maps, to begin the work of studying the stars at any part of the year. But for the description of the various constellations shown in the northern map for this month, he can refer to the account given for other months, when these constellations were visible, but differently placed.

The case is different with the southern stars (p. 205). These change all the year round,—*not* like the northern stars by merely circling round the pole, changing in position only as the hand of a clock does,—but new constellations coming constantly into view until the circuit of the year has been completed.

Yet we shall not have occasion this month for any lengthened descriptions, even of the southern stars. It has been for this reason that I selected this month for the account I have given of the real nature of the stars in the Plough. It seems to me, indeed, that merely to learn the stars is little, unless we know what they are. Then only have the glories of the starlit heavens their real meaning for us.

The chief ecliptical sign this month is Aquarius, the Water bearer, though the tail of the Sea-goat has not yet passed very far toward the west of the southern or central line of our monthly map. Although many say they can see nothing in this constellation to suggest the idea of a man carrying a water-jar, I think that no very lively imagination is required to portray such a figure among the stars. The man himself, indeed,

Fig. 32.—Part of Aquarius.

is wanting; but that is a detail: the water-can and the streams are there. The jar is formed by the stars η, ζ, π, γ, and α, as shown in Fig. 32. I am not quite sure whether originally the mouth of the jar may not have been fancied at α, and the handle at η. At present the jar, as you see in the southern map, comes horizontally to the south, and it matters little which end of the jar we suppose to be the mouth. But some four thousand years ago (and the constellation is at least six thousand years old), it came to the south with the end $\eta$ considerably higher than the end $a$; and as the idea was always that of a man pouring out water, I think the lower end of the jar was probably regarded as the mouth. You can easily see that the set of stars would serve either way—perhaps rather better the old way (as I suppose) than as in Fig. 32; for $\eta$ and $\zeta$ mark rather a stem than an opening, whereas the two stars $a$ and 32 (if not $o$ also) as in Fig. 33, would serve to represent the open mouth of a jar. Both ways the stars $\pi$ and $\gamma$ would correspond to the body of the jar. The streams are not shown in the map, because formed of small stars. Nor could they easily be presented, except in a large picture. But if you look attentively, you will see in the sky itself two streams, extending from below the star (rather from below $a$ than from below $\eta$, by the way), one passing windingly toward the star Fomalhaut,—the mouth of the Southern Fish,—the other flowing windingly over the Sea-goat, and thence along what is now called the Crane (Grus), a set of stars unquestionably belonging to the old water streams of Aquarius.

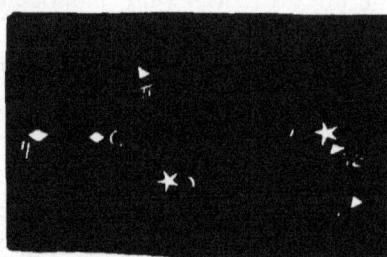

Fig. 33.—Part of Aquarius.

The sun in his annual motion passes the point of the ecliptic marked ♓, or, in technical terms, enters the sign Pisces on or about February 18

Little need be said about the remaining constellations visible toward the south. Piscis Australis, or "the Southern Fish," is chiefly remarkable for the bright star Fomalhaut in the fish's mouth. It may interest you to learn that the Arabs, before they learned the Greek constellations, called the Southern Fish "the First Frog;" a part of Cetus (the Whale), which figures toward the south next month, being called the "Second Frog."

In the east (p. 208), Andromeda and Aries are the chief constellations; but Cetus, whose head is shown in our eastern map, is worthy of notice, occupying a position near the horizon between the east and south-east. It has always seemed to me that the stars of this ancient constellation suggest the figure of some of those strange sea monsters, the Ichthyosaurians and Plesiosaurians, which are supposed to have passed away before man entered upon this terrestrial scene.

Taurus, Perseus, and Cassiopeia, with the Milky Way, extending from the north-eastern horizon to the point overhead, are also well worth observing at the present season of the year.

In the west (p. 209) the most noteworthy star-groups at present are Cygnus (the Falling Bird of the old astronomers), and Lyra (the Rising Bird), so called because the Lyre was commonly represented as grasped in the claws of a bird flying in a direction contrary to that in which the Swan was supposed to be moving. It will be interesting to the young observer to compare the steel-blue white of the brilliant Vega with the purer white of Altair. The Cross of Cygnus, formed by the five stars $a$, $\beta$, $\epsilon$, $\gamma$, and $\delta$ ($a$ and $\beta$ forming the upright and $\epsilon$ $\delta$ the cross-bar), is worth noting, and the complicated region of the Milky Way in this neighbourhood, now well seen on clear nights because raised so high above the horizon. The splendour of the Milky Way in the space between the stars $\gamma$, $\delta$, and $\beta$ of Cygnus is very remarkable. When this part of the heavens is examined with a good opera-glass an idea of the wealth of the heavens in *suns* is afforded; for where the naked eye perceives but a cloudy light the small powers even of an opera-glass reveal thousands of suns. In the gauging telescopes of the Herschels, hundreds of thousands of stars were seen as this part of the Milky Way was carried by the earth's motion across the telescopic field of view.

# STAR MAPS FOR OCTOBER.

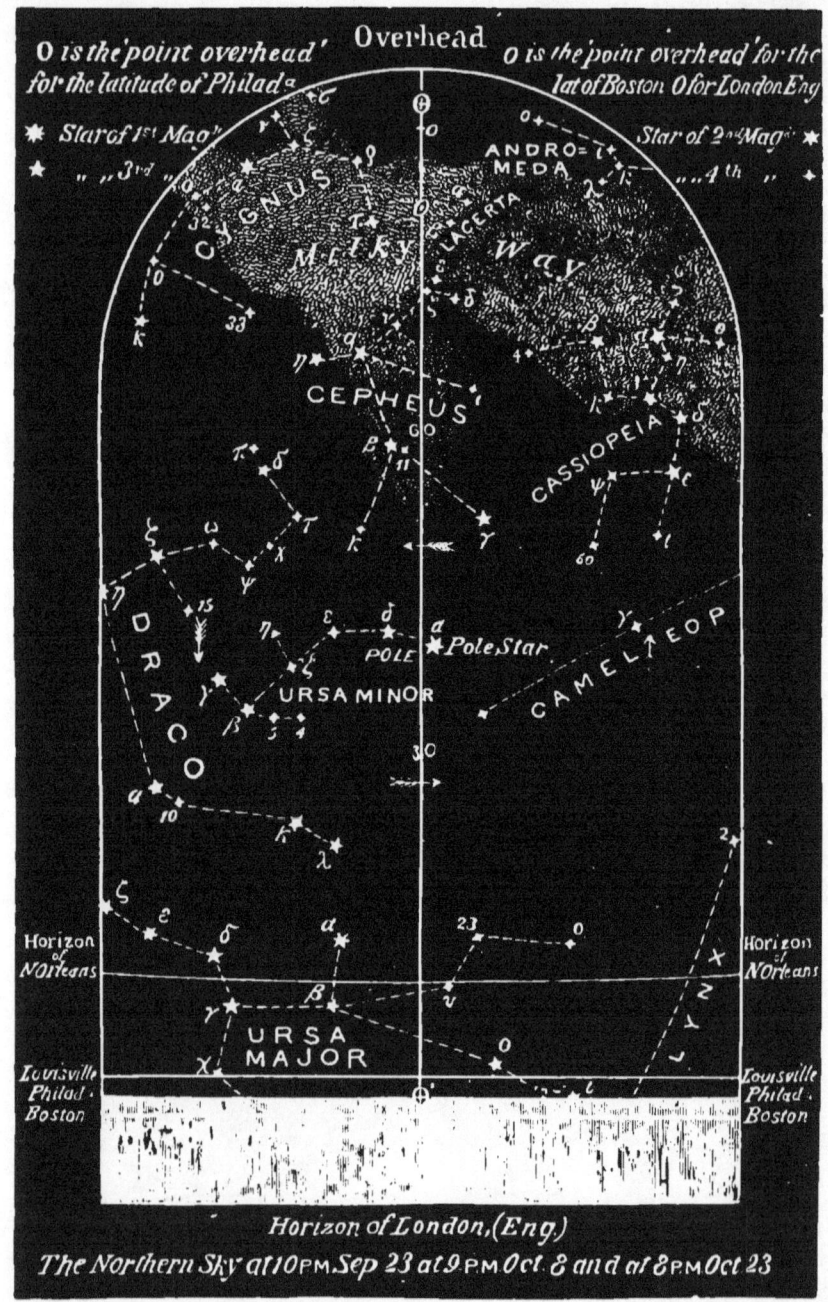

THE NORTHERN MAP FOR OCTOBER.

THE SOUTHERN MAP FOR OCTOBER.

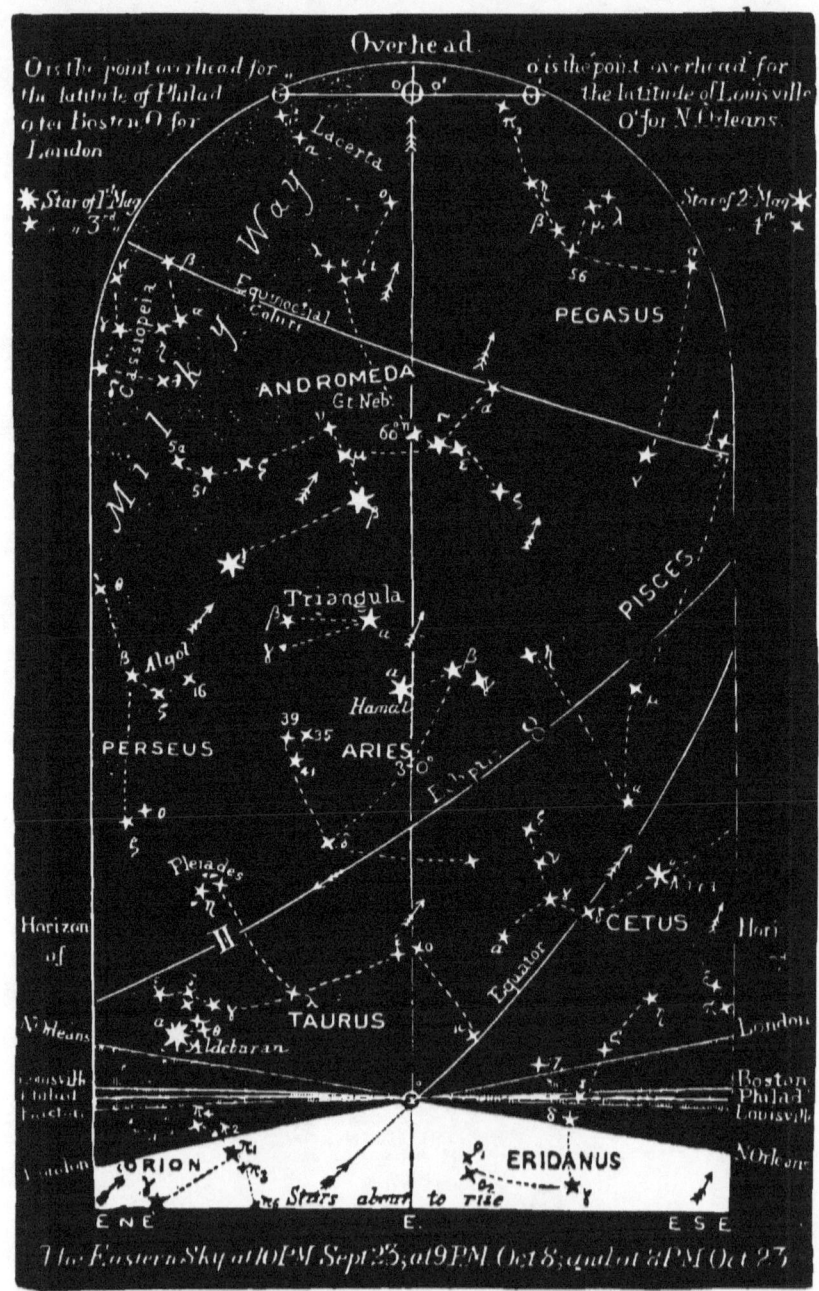

THE EASTERN MAP FOR OCTOBER.

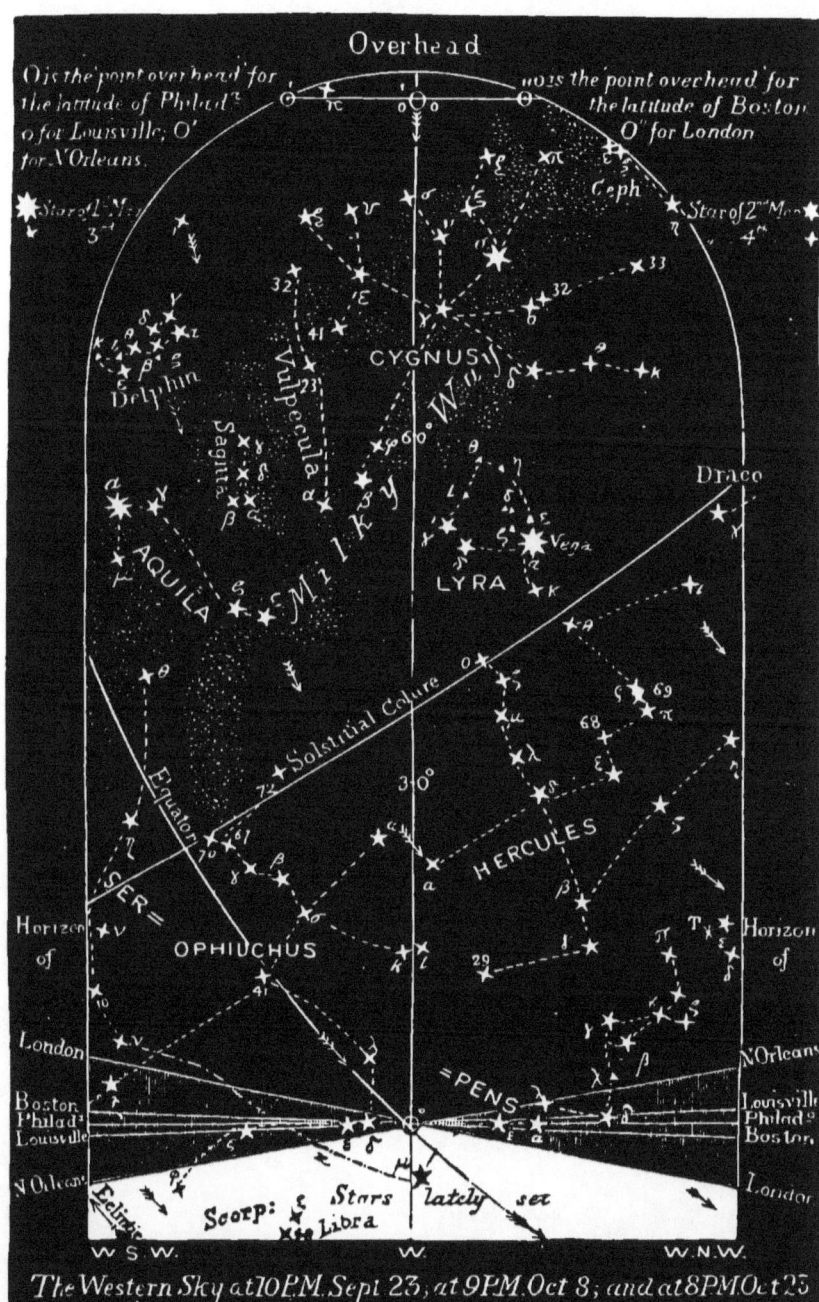

**THE WESTERN MAP FOR OCTOBER.**

# THE STARS FOR NOVEMBER.

The northern map (p. 220) explains itself, because we have already considered separately the constellations which appear in it. The Plough or Dipper is well placed for observation at this season for all places in America north of the latitude of Louisville, or not more than about two degrees south of it; but for places between this last-named latitude and that of New Orleans, a portion of the Plough is concealed from view. Nearly the whole constellation Ursa Major is seen in London, when due south below the pole; but the paws of the Great Bear are not seen in America at this time.

Turning to the southern skies (p. 221) for the month we find that the constellation Pisces, or "the Fishes," is the ecliptical constellation now ruling in the south. It is usually represented by two fishes tied together with a ribbon; one of the fishes has its tail at $\eta$, and its head close to Andromeda; the other has its head at $\gamma$ and $\beta$. You must be careful to distinguish the two fishes, Pisces, from the Southern Fish, Piscis Australis.

The constellation Pisces now includes the point marked $\Upsilon$, which is where the sign of the Ram begins, and was formerly occupied by this constellation; though, more anciently still, the Bull was the constellation occupying this part of the heavens. The Fishes belonged to the watery signs of the zodiac—Capricorn (the Sea-goat), Aquarius (the Water-pourer), and the Fishes, whose natural home is in the water. Below Aquarius you see another fish. Below Pisces there is the sea-monster Cetus, and close by Cetus, as you will see in the second southern chart for this month, is the watery sign Eridanus, named later as a river, but undoubtedly in the older system of the constellations represented as a great stream of water simply, something like the streams which were represented as flowing from the water-can of Aquarius.

I have already mentioned the old superstition of the astrologers that when the sun and moon and the other five planets (for the sun and moon were planets in the old system of astronomy) were conjoined in the watery signs, or specially in Capricornus, the world would be destroyed by a flood. It is rather curious that the history of the Flood was, in a sense, portrayed among the constellations, which (when the figures were first formed) lay south of the equator, insomuch that some have gone so far as to suggest that the narrative of the Flood is an account in words of what was pictured in the older temples of the stars (on the walls below the dome-roof which sprang from the circle representing the equator).

The coincidences are curious enough to be worth noticing, though to many the natural thought will be that the zodiac temples represented on their walls a more ancient history of a flood, not that the history was a later explanation of zodiac temples made long before.

We have the Water-pourer casting streams of water downward from the equator, as explained last month, the waters rising until the uppermost of the fishes rose nearly to the equator (so it would have been pictured in the remote ages referred to); while the great sea-monster and the still heavier streams of Eridanus on one side, with the Sea-goat on the other, indicate the prevalence of the waters which had been poured by Aquarius over all things. Passing onward (see successively the southern maps for January, February, March, &c.), we come first to the great ship Argo, which was associated in the earliest ages with the Ark;

next is the Centaur, which again we find from early authorities was formerly depicted as a man (the hinder quarters of the horse forming the fore part, at present missing, of the great ship). This man was represented bearing a sacrifice toward the altar, Ara, from which the smoke of burning incense rose into the heavens. We know that Noah, when he went forth from the ark, built an altar, and took of every clean beast, and of every clean fowl, and offered burnt-offerings on the altar; and that the smoke of burning incense rose from the altar of Noah may be inferred from the words which immediately follow, in the authorized version of the Bible narrative: "The Lord smelled a sweet savour."

Next after the altar, or rather above it, and in fact in the smoke from the altar, is the bow of Sagittarius,—and corresponding with this we read that God, after the savour of the altar had reached Him, said: "I do set my bow in the cloud, and it shall come to pass, when I bring a cloud over the earth, that the bow shall be seen in the cloud." Close by the ship Argo, again, is the raven, perched on Hydra (the great Sea-serpent), represented in the old sculptures immersed in the waves of ocean on which the ark was floating. Orion was from time immemorial associated with Nimrod (the mighty hunter before the Lord) and acordingly has his dogs beside him; while the first vineyard and vintage may be supposed to be indicated by the cup, Crater. (It seems also that Virgo—close by Crater—was represented of old as bearing grapes, and to this day the star $\epsilon$ of the Virgin is called Vindemiatrix, or "the Lady Gathering Grapes.")

The constellation Pegasus, or "the Winged Horse," is a singular one for several reasons. There is not the slightest resemblance to a winged horse among the stars of the group; and as usually represented the winged half horse has his head downward, the neck joining the body at $a$ and extending to $\zeta$, etc. The constellation is easily recognized by the three bright stars $\beta$, $a$, and $\gamma$, which with $a$ of

Andromeda form what is commonly called the square of Pegasus; for α Andromeda was also, of old, a star of Pegasus—to wit, δ of this constellation. You will observe that the fourth letter of the Greek alphabet has no representative star, at present, in the constellation.

The sun in his annual course along the ecliptic passes the point ♈, or crosses the equator moving northward, on or about March 21st.

In the east (p. 224) the stars of Orion are rising. Above the head and shoulders of the Giant are the horns of the Bull; and above these again the constellation Perseus. The Milky Way runs nearly vertically along the left of these constellations, and athwart the constellation Cassiopeia, which is now nearly overhead.

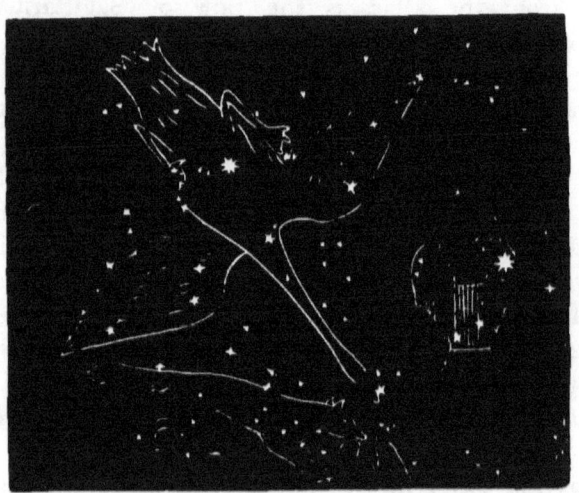

Fig. 34.—Cygnus, Lyra and Vulpecula.

In the west (p 225) we see the constellations of the Eagle and the Swan : all the original bird constellations are now in the west. The Lyre was one of these, being called the Rising Bird, while Cygnus (the Swan) was called the Falling Bird (Fig. 34).

The divided portion of the Milky Way is now well seen

in the west; specially noteworthy is the brightness of the branch on the right, where it crosses Cygnus, and the great diminution of the brightness as it approaches the constellation Ophiuchus, near the horizon,—in marked contrast with the comparative faintness of the branch on the left in Cygnus, and its great increase of brightness where it crosses the constellation of the Eagle.

# STAR MAPS FOR NOVEMBER.

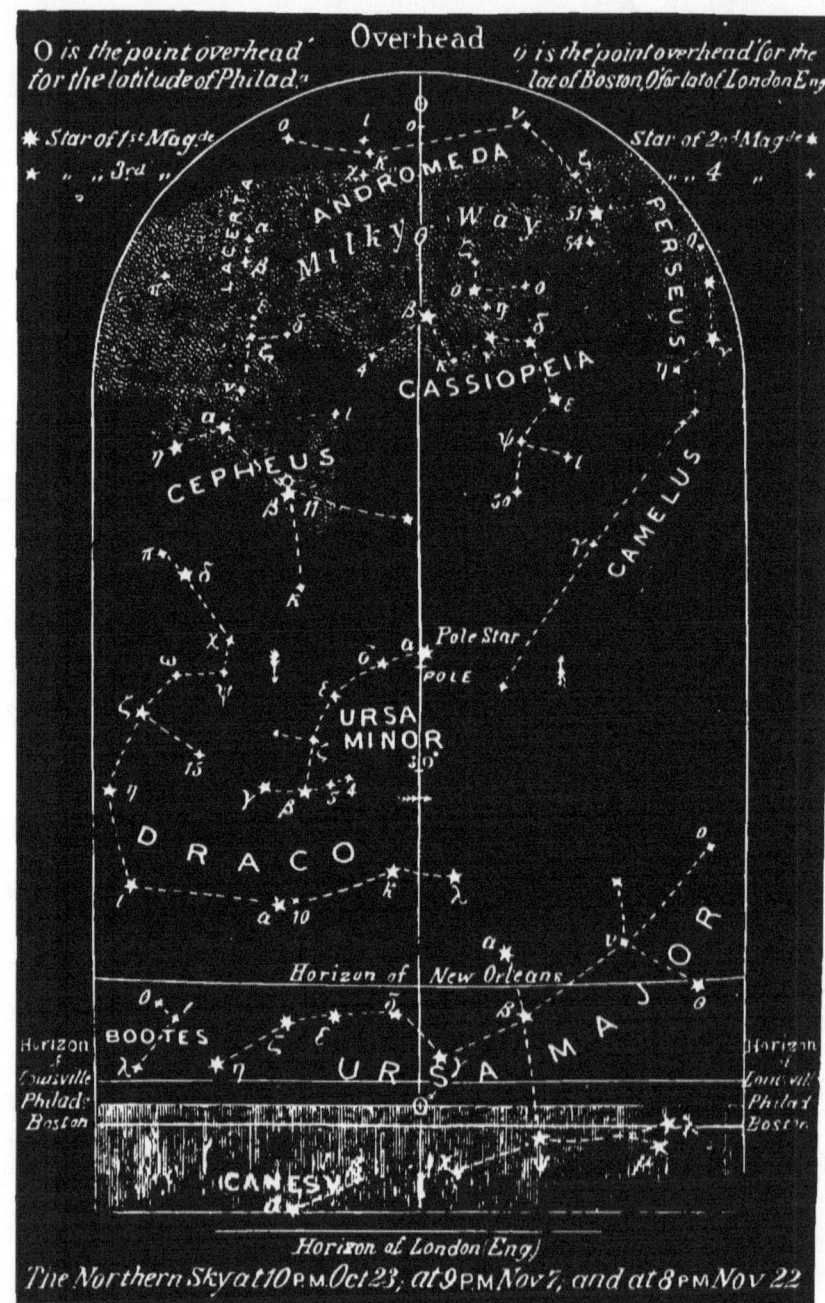

THE NORTHERN MAP FOR NOVEMBER.

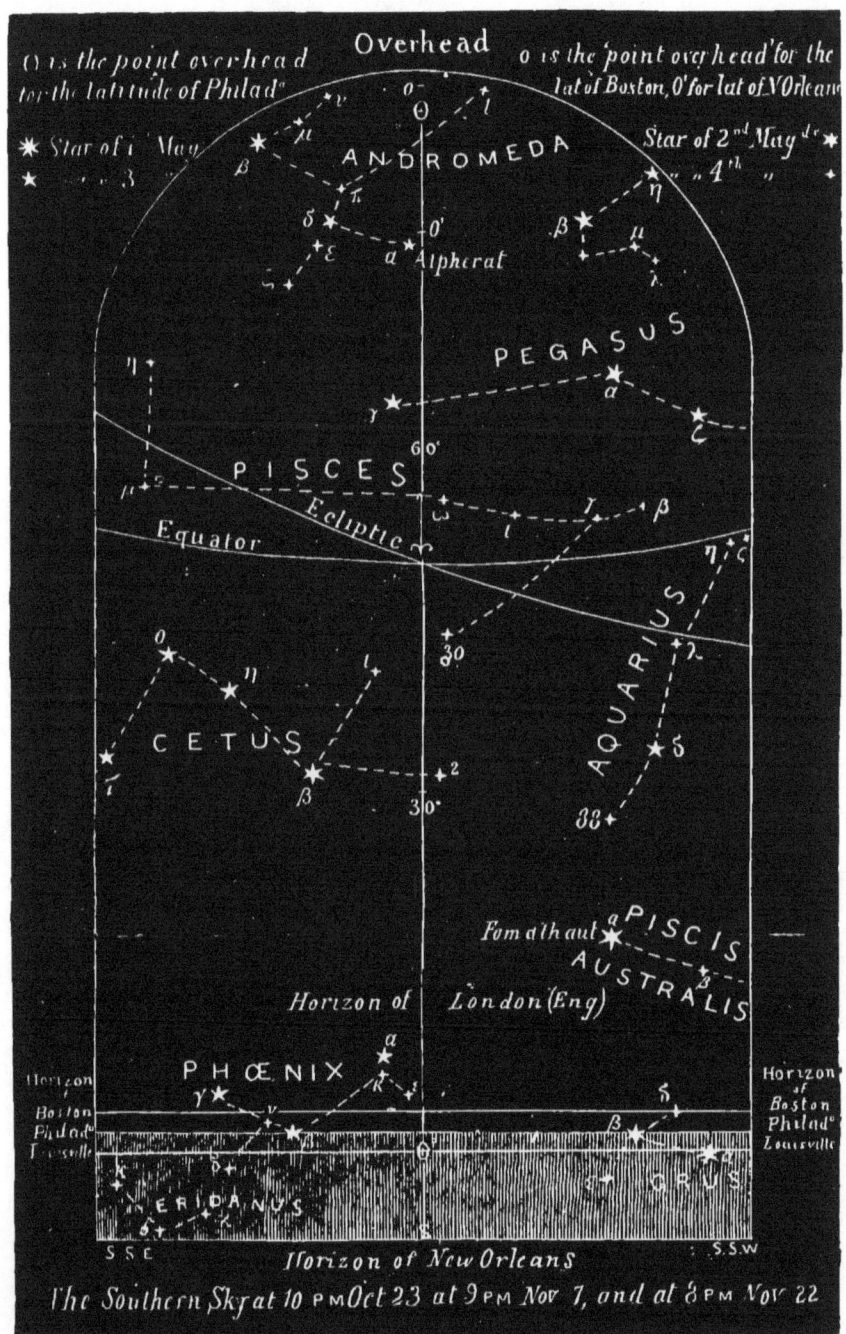

THE SOUTHERN MAP FOR NOVEMBER.

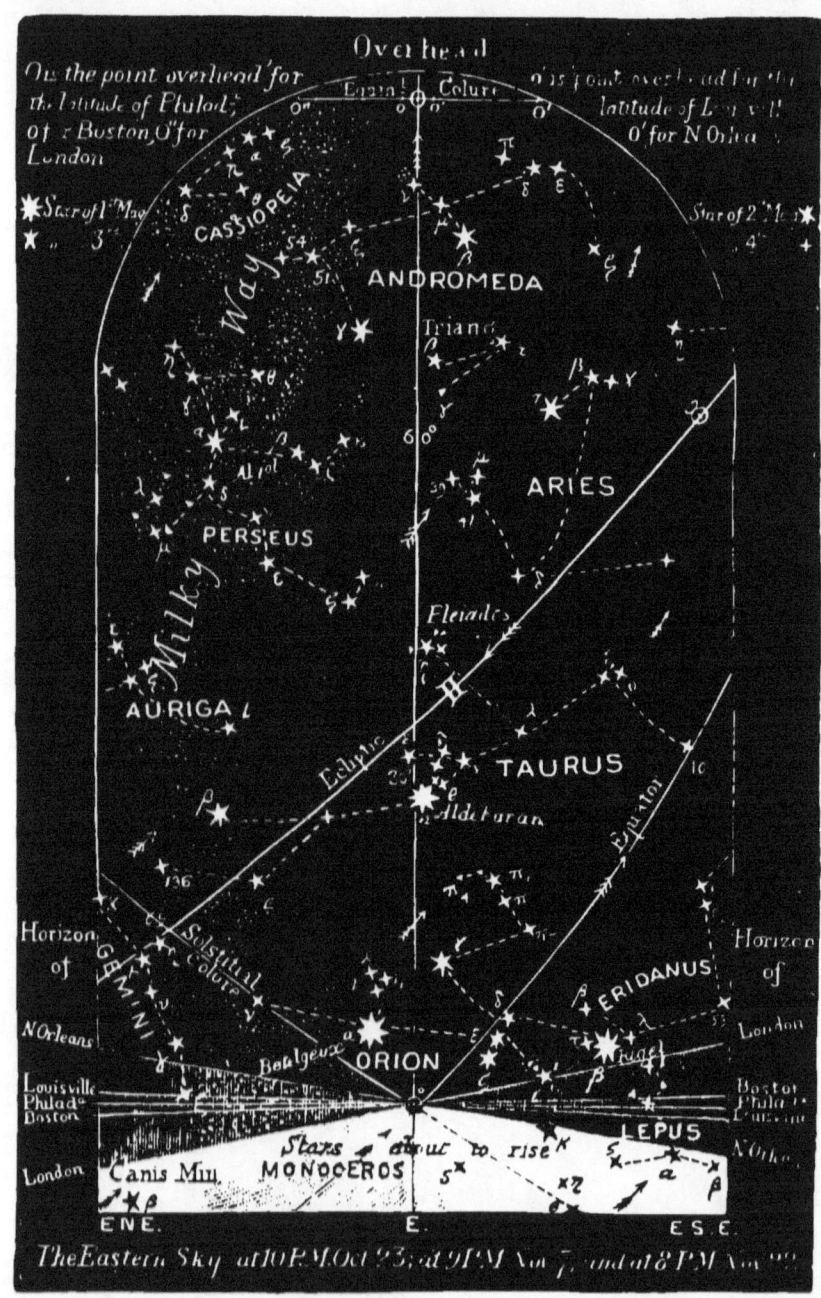

THE EASTERN MAP FOR NOVEMBER.

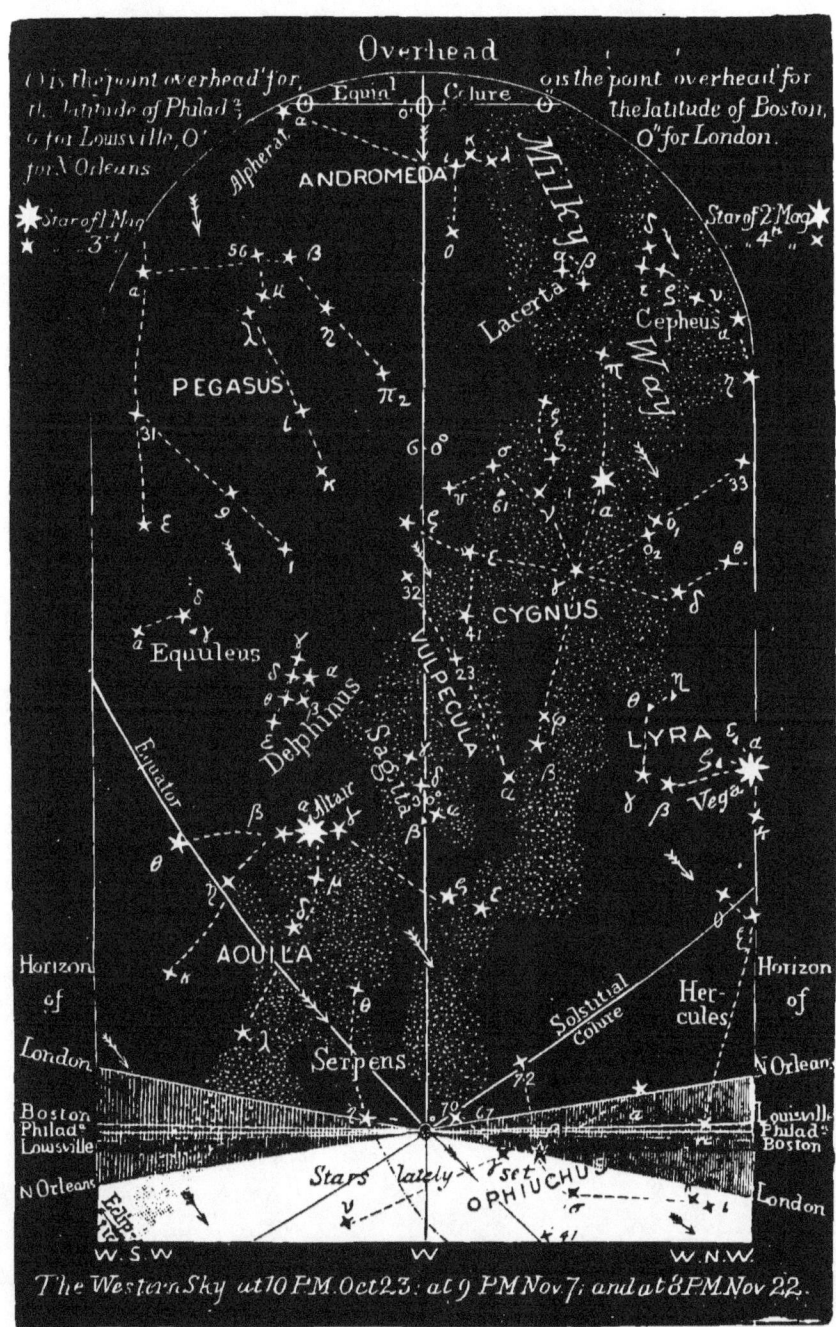

**THE WESTERN MAP FOR NOVEMBER.**

# THE STARS FOR DECEMBER.

THE northern map (p. 234) for December contains no new star-groups. It is only necessary to remark that this map makes the circuit of the northern heavens complete, the northern skies for the month following being those already shown in the first maps of our series.

Turning to the southern map (p. 235), the last of the southern series, we see that due south and high up toward the point overhead, lies the group of three stars, $a$, $\beta$, $\gamma$, forming the head of Aries (the Ram). The brightest of the three is called Hamal or "the Sheep." It is not easy to understand why this group was likened to a ram. One can just imagine the outline of a sheep's face looking toward the right (or west) as formed by the three stars $a$, $\beta$, and $\gamma$; but in the maps the face of the ram is turned the other way, looking toward the Bull, which lies on the left. This has been the idea for many centuries; for old Manilius wrote:

> First Aries, glorious in his golden wool,
> Looks back, and wonders at the mighty Bull.

Yet there is a tradition that in remoter times the Ram looked towards the west. Aries is one of the constellations of the zodiac, a set of twelve arranged as a zone or band round the heavens, along the middle of which runs the ecliptic, which is in fact the path of the sun. Formerly Aries was the first of the zodiacal constellations, but the same change which has shifted the pole from the Dragon to the Little Bear has shifted the Ram from his former position.

The sun in his course along the ecliptic crosses the point marked ♉, or enters the sign Taurus, on or about April 20th.

The stars $\mu$, 39, and 41, at one time formed a separate constellation called Musca (the Fly)—rather a large fly if Aries represents an ordinary ram.

Below the Ram there is the great straggling constellation called Cetus, or "the Whale." In reality it was intended, I suppose, to represent some imaginary sea monster (see fig. 11, p. 51); for the whale could hardly have been known to the astronomers who formed the older constellations. The group suggests rather an animal like the sea-serpent, rearing its head above water, than the great lumbering mass of a whale; and if the idea (see p. 199) that some recollection of the Enaliosaurian or long-necked (and long-named) reptiles was intended, is incorrect, then I imagine that the monster was no other than the crocodile. Slightly to modify the words of Shakespeare, we may say of this star group,

> It's almost in shape of a crocodile,
> By the mass and 'tis a crocodile, indeed.
> Methinks it's like a weasel.
> It is backed like a weasel.
> Or like a whale?
> Very like a whale.

For an account of "the Wonderful Star," see p. 52.

Above the Ram you will see the Triangles, one triangle formed of faint stars, the other of fairly conspicuous ones. The constellation Eridanus, or "the River Po," is seen to the left of the south, passing on a winding course, such as a river should follow, to the southern horizon. At places in latitude of New Orleans the bright star Achernar (of the first magnitude) shows where the river comes to an end. (Achernar signifies the latter part or end). The Bedouin Arabs call Eridanus "the Ostrich." The wide region almost bare of stars between Cetus and Eridanus is occupied by the modern constellations Fornax* (the Chemist's Furnace) and Sculptor* (the Sculptor's Workshop).

In the east (p. 238) the principal constellations are Canis Minor (the Lesser Dog), low down; Gemini (the Twins), next above; then again Auriga (the Charioteer), Fig. 35; and approaching the point overhead, the stars of Perseus (the Rescuer). Orion has passed over to the E.S.E, and above his head lie the principal stars of the Bull. The eastern skies show a singularly fine array of brilliant stars. Sirius and Procyon (the Greater and Lesser Dog-stars), Betelgeux and Rigel of Orion, Aldebaran, and Capella, are all first-magnitude stars; while among second-magnitude stars towards the east may be mentioned the three stars of Orion's belt—Bellatrix (Gamma of Orion), Castor and Pollux (Alpha and Beta, of Gemini)

Fig. 35.—Auriga.

The chief constellation in the western skies (p. 239) is Pegasus (the Winged Horse); above which is Andromeda (the Chained Lady); while somewhat below Pegasus we see on the left the stars of Aquarius, and on the right those of Cygnus. Low down in the west are the small constellations Equuleus and Delphinus.

* These Latin names are abbreviations for Fornax Chemica and Officina Sculptoria.

# STAR MAPS FOR DECEMBER.

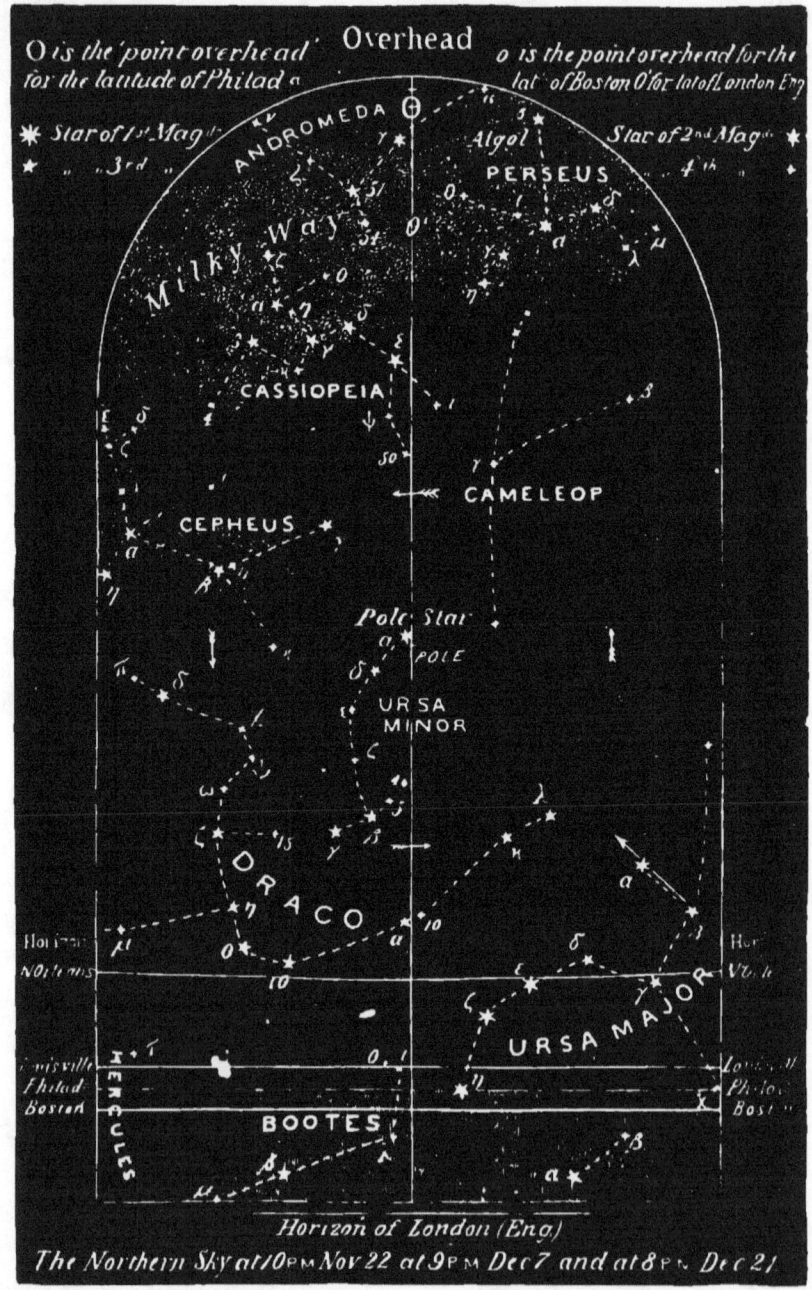

THE NORTHERN MAP FOR DECEMBER.

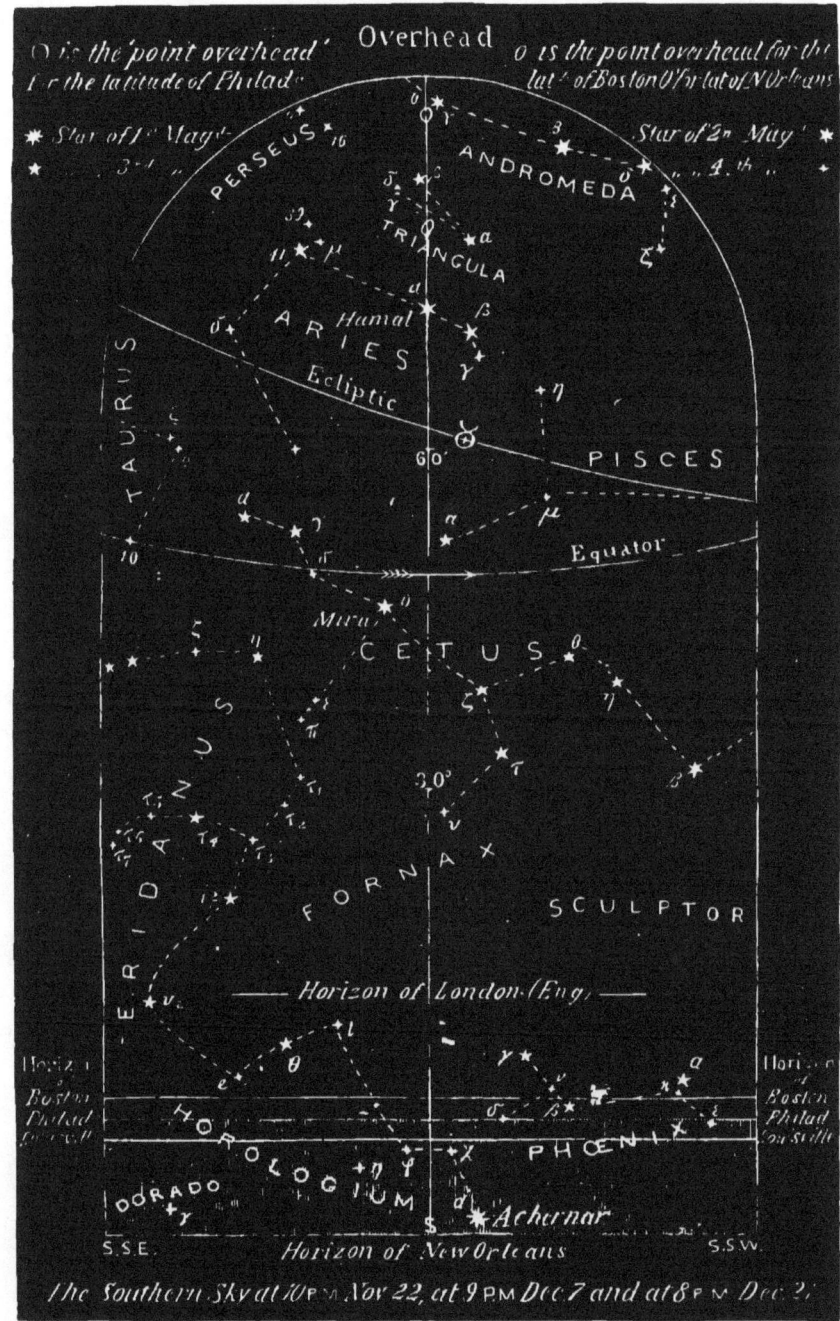

THE SOUTHERN MAP FOR DECEMBER.

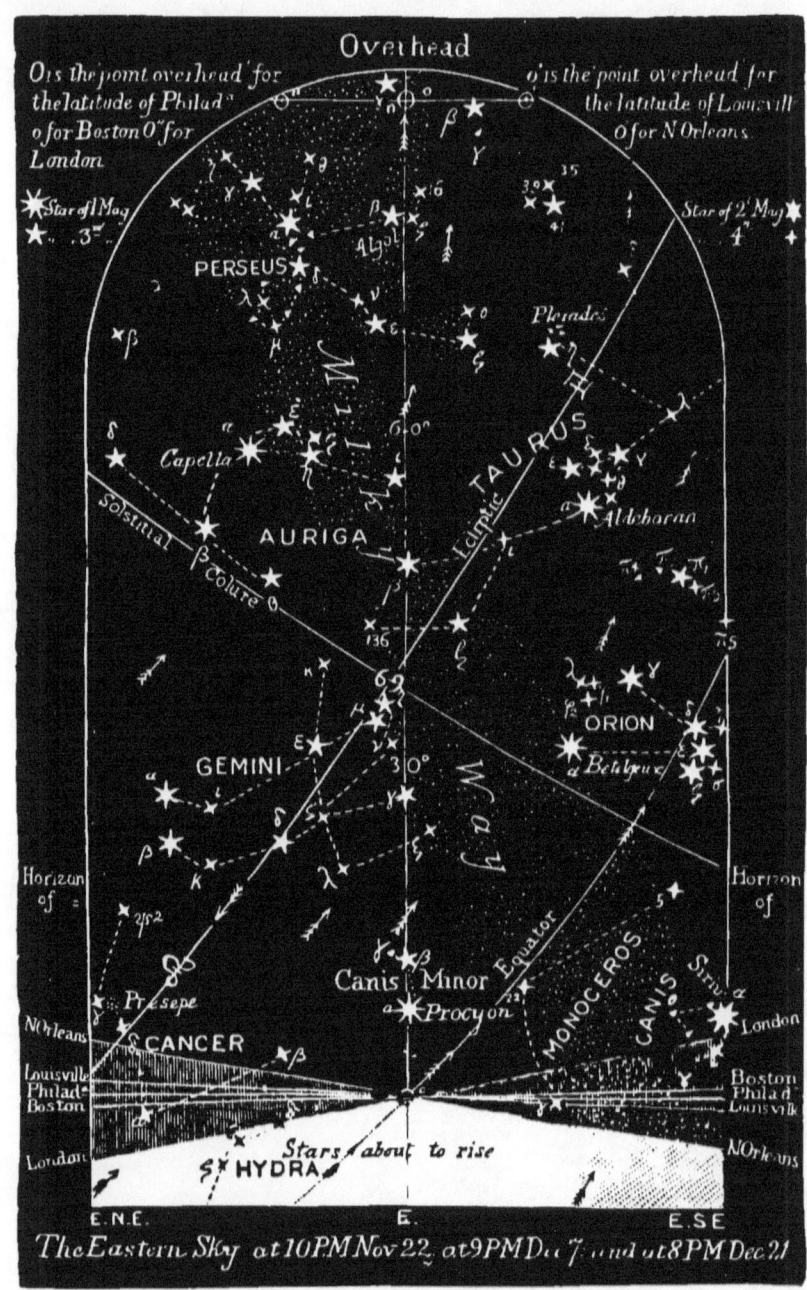

**THE EASTERN MAP FOR DECEMBER.**

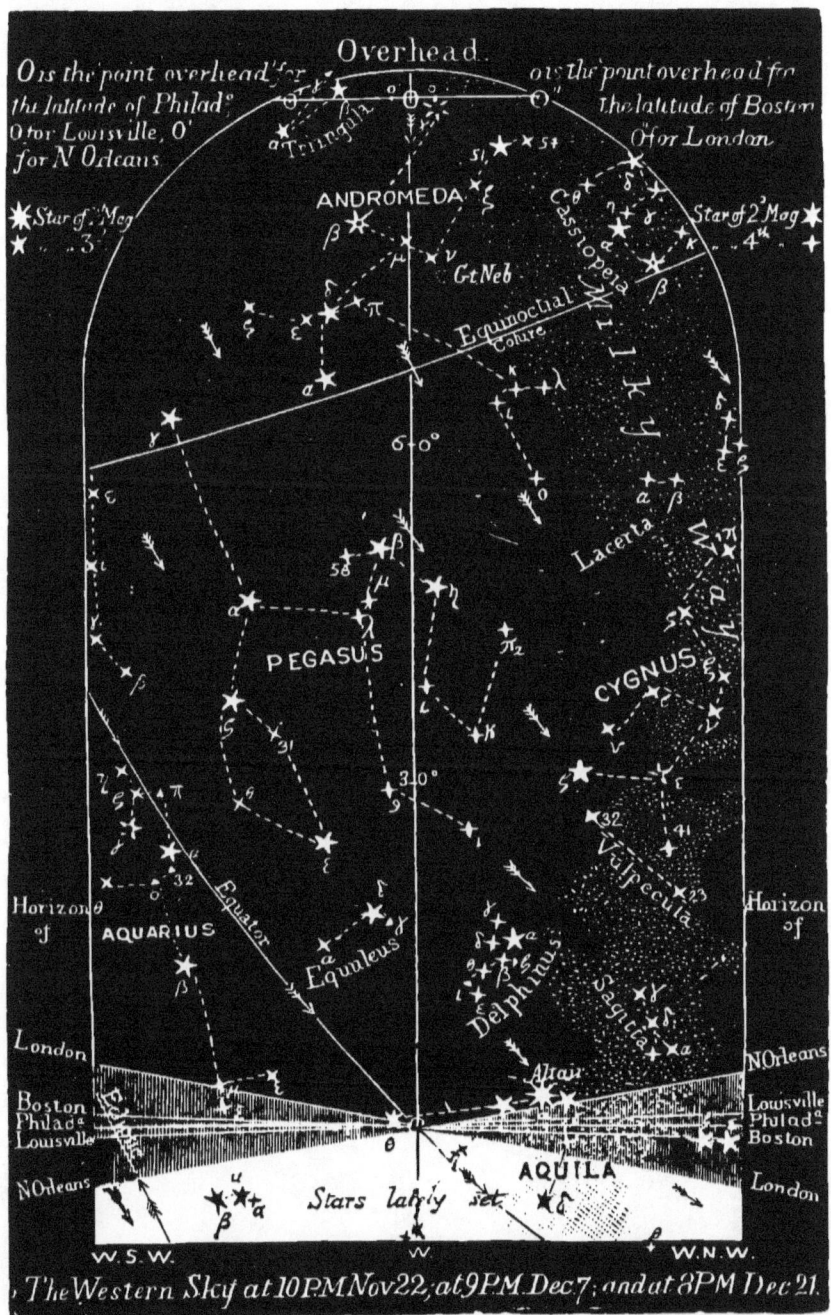

THE WESTERN MAP FOR DECEMBER.

www.ingramcontent.com/pod-product-compliance
Lightning Source LLC
Chambersburg PA
CBHW022008220426
43663CB00007B/1008